ONE HUNDRED YEARS OF
McKay-Dee
MOMENTS

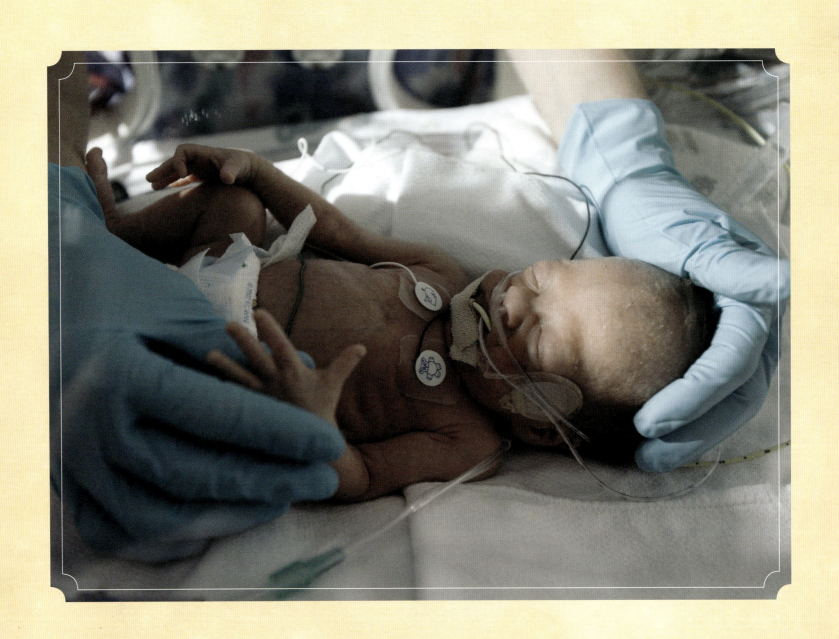

~ 1910 TO 2010 ~

ONE HUNDRED YEARS OF
McKay-Dee
MOMENTS

A CENTENNIAL JOURNEY OF
McKAY-DEE HOSPITAL CENTER

Intermountain℠
McKay-Dee Hospital Center
Healing for life

Intermountain McKay-Dee Hospital Center
4401 Harrison Boulevard ~ Ogden, UT 84403
801.627.2800 ~ www.intermountainhealthcare.org

One hundred years of McKay-Dee Moments ~ 1910–2010

Library of Congress Cataloging-in-Publication Data
Intermountain McKay-Dee Hospital Center
© 2010 with Resources

ISBN 978-1-4507-0551-6

Published by:
Timothy T. Pehrson, *CEO Intermountain Urban North Region & CEO Intermountain McKay-Dee Hospital Center*

Chris L. Dallin, *Director Public Relations, Media and Business Development, Intermountain McKay-Dee Hospital Center*

Acknowledgements:
Intermountain McKay-Dee Hospital Senior Management
Timothy T. Pehrson, Chief Executive Officer; Richard C. Arbogast, MD, Chief Medical Officer; Greg Blackburn, Operations Officer; Ruth Brockman, Operations Officer; Karen Burnett, Regional Director, Human Resources; Chris L. Dallin, Regional Director, Public Relations; Mike Hatch, Regional Director, Planning/Development; Bonnie Jacklin, Regional Chief Nursing Officer; Trever Porter, Director of Financial Planning; Doug Smith, Regional Chief Financial Officer; Cathleen Sparrow, Executive Director, McKay-Dee Hospital Foundation

Public Relations Department
Chris L. Dallin, Director; Breein Clark, Outreach Coordinator, 100-Year Anniversary; Nicholas Dragon, Web Strategy Specialist; Debra Farka, Marketing Manager; Scott Hayes, Outreach Coordinator; Jeremy Holt, Senior Writer/Graphic Designer; Tim Kendell, Professional Relations Manager; Lori Morris, Administrative Assistant

McKay-Dee Hospital Foundation
Cathleen Sparrow, Director; Kassi Bybee, Development Officer; Michelle Darrington, Development Assistant; Noellee Shaw, Development Officer; Ellen Snyder, Development Assistant

Special Acknowledgements:
John Grima, (former) Senior Planner, Intermountain McKay-Dee Hospital Center, Editing, Fact Checking; Jenifer Nii, Writer Intermountain Healthcare, Editing; Tom Vitelli, Assistant Vice President, Marketing, Intermountain Healthcare, Editing; McKay-Dee Hospital Human Resources, Editing and Review; Tami Martinez, Editing and Rewrites

Produced by:
Haight Handy Communications, LLC ~ Layton, Utah
David F. Haight, *Photography and Image Preparation;*
Stephen G. Handy, *Research, Interviews, Writing and Project Management;* Maralee Nelson, *Graphic Design;*
Caroll Shreeve, *Research, Interviews and Transcription, Writing and Text Preparation*

Printed in the USA by:
Taylor Publishing Company ~ Dallas, Texas

Contents

❖ DEDICATION ❖

Over the past 100 years, McKay-Dee Hospital Center has become much more than just an ordinary facility. The hours spent, the lives dedicated, and all that has been invested have truly made this hospital the memorial the Dee family always intended it to be. It is a reminder of good in the world, it is a place for hard work in the hardest of situations, and it is a place for healing.

THE CHURCH OF JESUS CHRIST OF Latter-day Saints is proud of its role in the history of this facility and its growth over the years. The hospital was founded by Annie Dee in 1910 following her husband's death by pneumonia. She was determined to help relieve suffering and to care for the sick people of the state, and she dedicated the hospital as a memorial to her late husband, Thomas Duncombe Dee, by naming it the Thomas D. Dee Memorial Hospital.

Four years after its founding, the hospital ran into financial difficulties. It was an expensive undertaking for the family, and they found they were unable to fully keep up with the demands. The family was unwilling to let the project die, so they approached their family friend, David O. McKay, who was a member of the Quorum of the Twelve Apostles of The Church of Jesus Christ of Latter-day Saints at the time. Because of his close ties to the Ogden area, he agreed to help, and through his influence and the assistance of other Church members, a financial solution was found, and the hospital was saved.

With the help and support of the LDS Church, the Dee Hospital was able to continue to grow and progress, and eventually, in 1969, it became the McKay-Dee Hospital with the construction of a new building. David O. McKay, who was now 93 and president of the LDS Church, was present for the 1966 ground-breaking of the new hospital building that bore his and the Dee family names. In 1969, he attended the dedication, although, at age 95 he was in very poor health and could not even leave his vehicle.

Through the years, members of the Dee family have continued to be strongly and deeply involved with the care and keeping of the hospital and what it stands for. Several family members have served on the hospital's board, and many have offered their assistance to the hospital and helped meet its needs in many generous ways.

The McKay-Dee Hospital has served many purposes; it has not been just a place to heal the sick. The Dee Hospital School of Nursing started with the beginning of the hospital in 1910 and graduated more than 700 nurses during the time it was open. The invaluable contributions to the health of Northern Utah by the nurses who were graduated from the school will long be remembered by the community. In 1955, the school was phased out and the students were integrated into a nursing program at Weber College, which, now as a university, continues to use the hospital for clinical experience.

In 1974, all LDS Church-supported hospitals and healthcare facilities became part of Intermountain Healthcare, a healthcare organization under which the McKay-Dee Hospital continues to thrive. Construction of yet another new hospital building was undertaken. As the study of medicine became more advanced, so did the hospital. McKay-Dee has continuously adapted to the needs of its patients, and the staff has constantly been committed to serving the community to the best of its ability with high-quality healthcare.

There have been many who have sacrificed much over the years in pursuit of Annie Dee's original dream. All who have been privileged to play a part in this hospital's proud history are happy to celebrate its 100-year anniversary. In addition to celebrating this significant milestone, we are also glad to have this time to remember. We remember the contributions of the Dee family, we remember the doctors and hospital workers who put in long hours giving the best possible care, we remember administrators who kept the hospital progressing, and we remember the patients who benefited from the hospital's care. We remember Annie Dee's vision, and as we remember, we recommit ourselves to the support of the McKay-Dee Hospital Center and its promising future. ❦

Elder Marlin K. Jensen
Historian & Recorder
The Church of Jesus Christ of Latter-day Saints

⇥ PREFACE ⇤

THIS BOOK COMMEMORATES AND CELEBRATES THE 100TH YEAR OF INTERMOUNTAIN McKAY-DEE HOSPITAL CENTER - ITS REMARKABLE FOUNDERS, ITS ONGOING FOCUS ON PROVIDING QUALITY HEALTHCARE, AND ITS COMMITMENT TO THE COMMUNITIES IT SERVES. WE PAY TRIBUTE TO THOSE INDIVIDUALS AND ORGANIZATIONS FOR WHOM THE HOSPITAL IS NAMED AND TO THEIR INVOLVEMENT IN MAKING HEALTHCARE SERVICES MORE GENERALLY AVAILABLE AND OF HIGHER QUALITY TO THE RESIDENTS OF NORTHERN UTAH. IN THE END, IT WAS THEIR VISION AND DETERMINATION THAT PAVED THE WAY FOR DOCTORS, NURSES, AND OTHER CAREGIVERS TO PRACTICE THEIR CRAFT THAT WOULD PROVIDE RELIEF AND HEALING TO SO MANY.

- Annie Taylor Dee and her descendants. It was Annie's vision and generosity that started the hospital in 1910. Their generous donations of time, energy, and philanthropic support have continued to enable McKay-Dee Hospital to offer quality healthcare.
- David O. McKay and The Church of Jesus Christ of Latter-day Saints. In 1915, David O. McKay was instrumental in working with the Dee family and The Church of Jesus Christ of Latter-day Saints to provide financial support and eventual ownership for the struggling hospital. His involvement over the years led decision-makers to name the first major replacement hospital after him in 1969.
- Intermountain Healthcare. A seismic evaluation in the mid-1990s revealed that the McKay-Dee Hospital could not withstand a significant earthquake. Those findings prompted Intermountain Healthcare's Board of Trustees to approve the construction of a new, $200 million facility. The Intermountain McKay-Dee Hospital Center opened in 2002.

This book also is dedicated to the many employees, physicians, community leaders, donors, volunteers, and others without whom this hospital could not have succeeded. To demonstrate such commitment so consistently over such a period of time is remarkable indeed and is a reflection of the character of this community.

With gratitude, we enter McKay-Dee's second century determined to honor their work and the hospital's proud legacy, from Annie Taylor Dee and David O. McKay to Intermountain Healthcare, by continuing to provide quality, compassionate healthcare. ⇜

Timothy T. Pehrson
CEO, Intermountain Urban North Region
& CEO Intermountain McKay-Dee Hospital Center

✦ MILESTONES ✦

~ *Tracing Our Progress 1910–1969* ~

1909 • Thomas D. Dee Memorial Hospital ground-breaking

1910 • Hospital dedication and opening

1913 • First blood transfusion
• Installation of Ogden's first X-ray machine

1915 • March 29, Dee family gave hospital to LDS Church

1917 • Nursing dormitory and school completed

1919 • Nitrous oxide gas anesthesia first used

1921 • Radiology department organized

1922 • First radium used in Northern Utah

1925 • First full-time staff radiologist pathologist

1927 • North wing constructed

1928 • Physiotherapy added

1929 • Pharmacy with full-time pharmacist

1932 • First oxygen tent used in Utah
• Capitol Street parking lot given by Drs. Ezra and Clark Rich

1937 • Central Service enabled centralized preparation of equipment and supplies

1938 • Pediatrics division opened

1942 • Separate Pathology and Radiology departments

1944 • Penicillin first administered

1946 • Ogden Surgical Society (later Ogden Surgical-Medical Society) formed

1948 • First outpatient clinics established

1952–54 • New medical staff constitution and bylaws

1953 • Hospital Anesthesia department employed physician-anesthesiologists
• Daycare established for employees' children

1953–63 • Psychiatry division established, the first in a Utah general hospital
• Post-surgery Recovery Room opened
• Physical Therapy department
• Occupational Therapy department
• Nuclear Medicine Laboratory

• Personnel department
• In-service department for continuing education
• Childbirth education classes
• Emergency Room separate from surgery
• Outpatient department
• Polio Ward equipped with iron lung
• Diagnostic and Convalescent Unit
• Community and Patient Relations department
• Social Services department

1955 • School of Nursing merged with Weber State College
• Radium Therapy begun on a regular basis
• Surgery and Delivery Room air-conditioned
• Living quarters for residents and families

1958 • Volunteer Auxiliary established

1959 • Intensive Care Unit received critical patients

1963 • Home Care Nursing, Utah's first hospital-based home healthcare

1966 • First in Utah, second in U.S., 24-hour physician coverage of Emergency Room
• January, bids presented for constructing new hospital at 3939 Harrison Boulevard
• April 23, ground-breaking for new David O. McKay Hospital at 3939 Harrison Boulevard

1968 • Hospital assets grew from $110,000 in 1910 to $4,301,627
• First hospital foundation in Utah created, the McKay-Dee Hospital Foundation, to raise funds for new hospital

1969 • July 9, dedication of the new David O. McKay Hospital
• July 12, David O. McKay Hospital, an acute facility, opened
• First 145 patients transferred from the Thomas D. Dee Memorial Hospital

→ MILESTONES ←

~ *Tracing Our Progress 1969–2002* ~

1970 • Bids opened for Dee wing
   • First Intensive Care Nursery in Northern Utah
   • June 30, the Dee officially closed and tuberculosis patients were transferred to Weber County Hospital

1971 • New Thomas D. Dee Memorial Hospital wing, convalescent/rehabilitation center, opened
   • Both hospitals became known as McKay-Dee Hospital Center, not-for-profit 380-bed hospital
   • First coronary artery bypass operation performed
   • McKay-Dee chosen for Utah's first family practice residency
   • Helicopter landing pad opens near the Emergency Room
   • Cardiac Surgery Unit opened
   • McKay-Dee became first Utah hospital accredited by Joint Commission on Accreditation of Hospitals

1972 • The Dee Hospital is demolished

1974 • New nurses and labor rooms opened
   • LDS Church returned 15 hospitals, including McKay-Dee Hospital, to communities served; creation of Intermountain Healthcare
   • Rehab Center at McKay-Dee opened

1975 • Ultrasound Examination Unit installed

1977 • Installation of hospital's first full-body scanner

1979 • First CT Scanner installed

1980 • Stewart Rehabilitation Center opened

1981 • Outpatient Surgical Center opened
   • Laser instrument put into use in Operating Room
   • Psychological Outpatient and Crisis Intervention instituted

1983 • All Intensive Care Units expanded
   • 174 open-heart procedures (double the previous year)

1985–88 • Major remodel and expansion projects

1986 • Pediatric Rehabilitation Center opened
   • Outpatient Surgical Center and offices opened

1987 • McKay-Dee Institute for Behavioral Health began operations

1990 • 2,000 employees, 428 beds (licensed), 283 beds

1991 • MRI scanner in operation

1997 • Decision to build new McKay-Dee Hospital at 4401 Harrison Boulevard

1999 • Construction begun on new McKay-Dee Hospital
   • Children's Health Connection instituted

2000 • 155,000 monthly newborn web pages viewed
   • Pharmacy robot operational
   • Emergency Department handled 48,000 patient visits
   • Intermountain Healthcare named No. 1 Healthcare System (of 578 systems) in U.S. by Chicago-based SMG

2001 • New Cancer Center operational
   • First Jaynie Nye Memorial Benefit Concert
   • Web-based imaging display (PACS) allows short- and long-term storage, retrieval, management, distribution and presentation of images and documents on all hospital computers
   • Intensive Care Unit expanded
   • Local foundations, individuals, and 1,325 employees donate $15.9 million to new hospital's healing environment

✦ MILESTONES ✦

~ *Celebrating 100 Years 2002–2010* ~

2002 • Intermountain McKay-Dee Hospital Center dedicated March 20
    • 150 patients moved from McKay-Dee Hospital Center to the new facility on March 25
    • Grand piano for lobby music donated by the Stewart Education Foundation and Piano Guild organized by the McKay-Dee Hospital Foundation
    • Dr. W. C. Swanson Family Foundation Child Development Center for children of employees opened
    • Acquired linear accelerator, which delivers a uniform dose of high-energy X-ray to the region of a cancer patient's tumor while sparing surrounding healthy tissue
    • Brachytherapy equipment (low dose rate) for oncology acquired

2003 • Life Flight became 24-hour operation
    • Emergency Department remodel added 10 beds

2004 • Patient Education and Care Channel System initiated

2005 • First 64-"slice" CT Scanner installed
    • Angel Watch Program instituted
    • Brachytherapy equipment (high dose rate) for oncology acquired
    • Women's Council refurbished guest houses
    • Bedside coding equipment installed
    • Emergency Department capacity increased

2006 • Medical Office Building wing added
    • SonoCine mammogram ultrasound equipment tested and installed

2007 • Hospital certified as primary stroke center
    • Classic Race (5K, 10K, walk) management began, inherited from *Standard-Examiner*
    • Huntsman Cancer Center collaboration began
    • Stewart Rehab remodeling combined outpatient services

2008 • Linear Accelerator for radiation therapy installed
    • Navigator Cancer Program, patient treatment system began

2009 • U.S. President Barack Obama and other national leaders declare Intermountain Healthcare one of country's best healthcare systems
    • McKay-Dee Hospital Foundation broke ground for Annie Taylor Dee Guest Home
    • Psychiatry Unit added 12 beds

2010 • Hospital reaccredited by American College of Surgeons Commission on Cancer
    • DaVinci Surgical Robot installed
    • Intermountain McKay-Dee Hospital Center celebrates 100 years of service
    • Dedication and opening of Annie Taylor Dee Guest Home
    • Named Top 100 Hospital by Thomson Reuters

PART ONE

100 YEARS *of* HOSPITAL FACILITIES

ANNIE TAYLOR DEE'S VISION *Lives On*

THE EXTRAORDINARY HISTORY OF THE DEE HOSPITAL IS INTERWOVEN WITH THE LIFE STORIES OF THE DEE FAMILY. FOR 100 YEARS, THE COMMUNITY OF OGDEN, UTAH, HAS BENEFITED FROM ANNIE TAYLOR DEE'S GENEROSITY AND STRENGTH IN THE FACE OF TRAGEDY.

In 1894, an immigrant couple, Thomas Duncombe and Annie Taylor Dee, suffered the loss of their 21-year-old eldest son, Thomas Reese. As reported in *A Tradition of Caring*, a history of the Thomas D. Dee Memorial Hospital and McKay-Dee Hospital Center, 1910-1982, by Eleanor B. Moler, his appendectomy was performed on the family's dining room table because there was no hospital nearby. Tragically, the surgery was too late; Thomas' appendix had already ruptured. He died at home.

In July 1905, Annie's beloved husband, Thomas Duncombe Dee, contracted pneumonia after falling into the river near South Fork Canyon. He died on July 9, 1905, leaving Annie and her children, as well as the entire Weber County community, stunned at the passing of "Judge Dee," as he was affectionately known.

Having endured her son's loss, Annie's heartbreak was compounded at Thomas' passing. She faced the future with seven children to raise alone. In her grief, she resolved to honor her husband's memory with a hospital that would offer the best quality of compassionate medical care known in those days. For patient families with limited funds, Annie planned to pay for their care herself.

The Thomas D. Dee Memorial Hospital Association was incorporated. Annie and her children conveyed a three-acre tract of land to the association as a site for the hospital. Work began immediately.

One hundred years and three hospitals later, Annie Taylor Dee's vision has saved thousands of lives. Succeeding Dee generations continue to sustain her legacy through new Thomas D. Dee Memorial projects. This commemorative book celebrates that history and legacy. ⤸

Annie Taylor Dee was a woman of vision with an iron-willed commitment to memorializing her husband with an excellent hospital.

The THOMAS D. DEE
MEMORIAL HOSPITAL
✦ 1909 *to* 1970 ✦

THOMAS D. DEE AND OTHERS had purchased the Ogden City Water Works for $1 at a bankruptcy sale after "Eastern Capitalists," as they were called, allowed the system to fall into disrepair, as well as receivership. Dee and his associates planned to restore the system and turn it over to the city, according to various sources.

The morning after the 1905 Independence Day celebrations, as reported in *A Tradition of Caring*, Dee and two other civic-minded Ogden leaders went in search of additional water sources for the growing city. The three drove up a rough road through Ogden Canyon into Ogden Valley. During this adventure in the scorching summer heat, they left their vehicle frequently to survey springs and seeps and assess the flow of the Ogden River and its tributaries, intending to find a location for a future reservoir.

At some point, Dee fell into what the *Deseret News* described as "a branch of the Ogden River."

Two days later, Judge Dee developed pneumonia. In another two days, on July 9, 1905, with his beloved wife, Annie Taylor Dee, and their seven living children at his bedside, Thomas Duncombe Dee died at age 61. It was a

On July 10, 1909, as Annie Taylor Dee turned the first shovel of dirt to begin construction of a hospital in memory of her husband, we can only wonder what she was thinking. Could she have realized that her vision for a modern general hospital would, a hundred years later, see not one, but two successors counted among America's best community hospitals?

Above: Distinguished businessman and community leader Thomas D. Dee died at age 61 on July 9, 1905.

Right: In 1912, 60-year-old widow Annie Taylor Dee presented this photograph to her granddaughter Elizabeth (Elizabeth Shaw Stewart). The Dee Memorial Hospital had been in operation for two years.

With Love to Elizabeth From Grandma Dee
Nov 4th 1912

Above: Annie Taylor and Thomas Duncombe Dee enjoy a sleigh ride. This is one of the few photographs of them together.

Right: Remodeled Dee family home at 806 Washington Boulevard, Ogden, Utah.

Facing: Annie Taylor Dee and her seven children had their photograph taken for the cornerstone ceremony of the Thomas D. Dee Memorial Hospital, which was held on September 27, 1910. The photograph was among the memorabilia included in the time capsule. *Front, from left:* Rosabelle, Maude, Annie, and Elizabeth. *Rear, from left:* Florence, Margaret, Lawrence, and Edith.

devastating loss for Annie and her children.

By any measure of those times, Annie Taylor Dee proved herself a remarkable woman. Annie was born November 4, 1852, in Lostock Graham, Cheshire, England. She and her family converted to The Church of Jesus Christ of Latter-day Saints. Bound for Utah, Annie, then 7 years old, traveled 1,000 miles with her family in a wagon train captained by her father. They arrived in Great Salt Lake City on September 17, 1860. Little did she know that among the members of another wagon train traveling at the same time was 16-year-old Thomas Duncombe Dee.

Thomas and Annie were married in 1871 and made their home in Ogden, Utah. They had eight children. The eldest, Thomas Reese, was born in 1873 but died tragically at age 21 while undergoing surgery for a ruptured appendix. Maude Dee Porter later remarked about her late brother, "In the early years of his manhood, Reese passed away – a beautiful, valiant

spirit. His death left a void that nothing could fill" – true of both son and father, as reported in *A Tradition of Caring*.

Thomas Duncombe Dee engaged in numerous successful business enterprises with David Eccles and others. Dee and Eccles became involved in what later became Anderson Lumber Company and is now Stock Building Supply.

They began the Ogden Sugar Company and the Logan Sugar Company, which grew to become the Amalgamated Sugar Company. Dee was active in the First National Bank and the Ogden Savings Bank, which became First Security Corporation and is now Wells Fargo. He organized and was president of Utah Construction Company, which grew to become Utah International, according to *Weber County's History* by Richard Sadler and Richard C. Roberts.

Dee's record of community service rivaled that of his business dealings. He served as Ogden councilman and was elected justice of the peace, leading many to call him

"Judge Dee." He was a member of Utah's first State Board of Equalization and the Utah State Tax Commission, as reported in *Building A Dynasty*, the story of the Thomas D. Dee family by Eleanor B. Moler.

Dee was a self-educated man who'd had less than two years of formal schooling. He taught himself by reading the many books in his personal library. His love of books prompted him to serve as president of Ogden's first library.

It is no wonder then that he devoted his energies to supporting education in Ogden. He was associated with the Ogden School Board for 35 years and served eight years as president and in other civic capacities.

Given Dee's business and community service ties to the area, his untimely death in 1905 shook the community. According to newspaper accounts, American flags flew at half-staff, schools were let out for the day, and children lined the streets for the funeral procession.

Utah Gov. John S. Cutler spoke at the funeral, along with Joseph F. Smith, president of The Church of Jesus Christ of Latter-day Saints, who said, "I expect someday to have the pleasure of again meeting my friend and brother, Judge Dee, on the other side of this veil of tears."

Perhaps the most difficult period of Annie's life now began. Four of their children were young, still at home, and required care. Furthermore, while her husband left a significant estate, Annie encountered many difficulties in settling his affairs because he died without a will, according to *A Tradition of Caring*. Thinking back on the enormous load she carried, she later remarked: "I just never realized how much I depended on Thomas. He made decision-making so easy; his thoughts on every subject were so logical."

As reported in *A Tradition of Caring*, Annie explored numerous ways to memorialize her husband. Her friend and

Left: Robert S. Joyce, MD, was a doctor for the railroads and Dee family friend and confidant. He recommended a hospital to Annie as a fitting memorial to her husband. Dr. Joyce became the Dee's first chief of the medical staff.

Above: Maude Dee Porter was her mother's closest partner in the establishment of the Thomas D. Dee Memorial Hospital. She was 34 years old when construction began in 1909 and served as the hospital board's first secretary. She was intimately involved in its ownership transfer to the LDS Church in 1915.

personal physician, Robert S. Joyce, MD, encouraged her to build a hospital. At the time, the Ogden Medical and Surgical Hospital and the Japanese Hospital served Ogden residents. The Ogden Medical and Surgical Hospital had only six or eight private rooms for patients, and many felt that something more was needed to provide for the healthcare needs of the growing community. It was a daunting challenge. Annie's eldest daughter, Maude Dee Porter, later reflected: "This was a field entirely outside our knowledge or experience, but we made up for that in our sincerity of purpose."

A Tradition of Caring reports that they forged ahead and incorporated the Thomas D. Dee Memorial Hospital Association with Annie as president and Maude as secretary. Just a few days later, Annie conveyed to the association a three-acre site on the corner of Harrison Boulevard and 24th Street in Ogden. The name, purpose, and longevity of the Thomas D. Dee Memorial Hospital Association were listed in the articles of incorporation:

I. The association shall be known as Thomas D. Dee Memorial Hospital Association.

II. It shall exist for one hundred years from the date of incorporation.

III. It is created for the purpose of maintaining, operating and conducting hospitals and other institutions for the care and treatment of sick, wounded, injured or infirm persons; of maintaining schools and other places for the education and training of nurses; of acquiring, holding, owning and controlling suitable ground and structures to carry out the objects of this corporation, with power to receive from any source whatever gifts, donations, devises (sic) and bequests of real and personal property, for the use and benefit of the corporation.

Annie and her advisors, including Dr. Joyce, studied hospital designs and operations in the United States and even Europe.

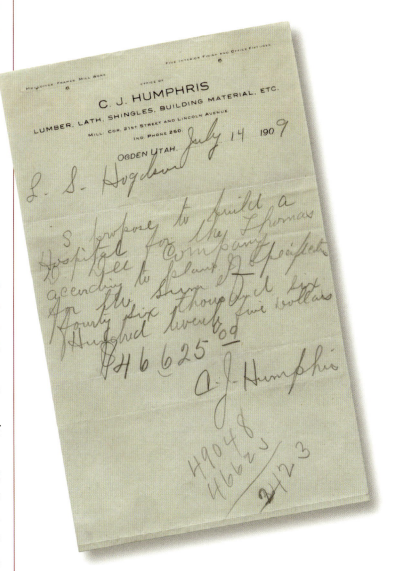

Inset: Although the handwritten contract by C.J. Humphris to architect L.S. Hodgson lists the construction estimate as $46,625, significant change orders must have occurred because later records indicate the complete cost of the unfurnished structure was actually $75,000. Another $25,000 was required for furnishings, which was in part covered by community donations. The hospital was built in roughly a year and a half.

The *Ogden Morning Examiner*'s report on the ground-breaking ceremony, held July 10, 1909, described the building:

> The structure will be one of the most modern of its kind in the United States. Everything will be complete and perfect in its detail, such as heating, lighting, ventilation, signal system, etc. The main building will be built of red brick, 60 feet by 148 feet, and four stories and basement, and will have wards for the accommodation of 100 patients. It will be erected in the center of a three and a half acre tract of land.

> The building will cost about $75,000 and the furnishings and equipment will cost an additional $25,000. In connection with the building of the main structure, a large boiler house and laundry will also be constructed. From this will be furnished the heat, electric light, and power for the large elevator in the center of the building.

Above: The foundation and walls are clearly visible in this photograph taken at the cornerstone ceremony for the Thomas D. Dee Memorial Hospital on September 27, 1910. The cornerstone was set on the building's northwest corner and included a time capsule that was opened in the early 1970s after the Dee was demolished.

Construction progressed rapidly. At a cornerstone ceremony held September 27, portraits of Thomas D. Dee and Annie Taylor Dee and their children were buried in a time capsule, along with a typewritten history of the family and its reasons for building the hospital; a copy of the Articles of Incorporation; copies of the *Deseret Evening News*, *Salt Lake Herald Republican*, and *Ogden Morning Examiner*; clippings from various papers praising Annie; a scalpel, scissors, and forceps from Dr. Joyce; two 1905 Liberty Head nickels; and cards of 43 people attending the ceremony, as well as souvenir postcards of Ogden and Salt Lake City. On December 29, 1910, a proud and happy Annie formally presented the hospital to the public in extensive ceremonies held on the building's fourth floor. Annie said:

"Our family feels both thankful and pleased to see this fruition of our desires, because we are convinced that in no other way could we more honor the memory of our beloved husband and father than in tendering this hospital to the people of the community for whom he so loved and among whom he spent practically his entire life."

In an article referred to in *A Tradition of Caring*, Ogden Mayor William Glasmann stated, "When those who erected this beautiful monument first conceived the idea, it must have been that the memory of Judge Dee was dear to them. It must have been that they remembered the kind and loving husband, the generous and indulgent father."

The mayor continued, "The gift, as it stands, is absolute to the people. There are no strings on it, excepting that if you cease to use it for what it has been dedicated, it reverts back to the family."

Finally, he made an appeal for members of the community to be generous with their philanthropy toward the hospital and shared his hope for its future: "Mrs. Dee has made a beginning and this $100,000 building may eventually develop into a $1 million plant and we may have in our midst the greatest medical and surgical institution in the entire West."

Coincidentally, the current McKay-Dee Hospital Center at 4401 Harrison Boulevard was built on land owned by Mayor Glasmann's descendants.

Two days after the presentation, 15 patients from the Ogden Medical and Surgical Hospital were transferred to what affectionately came to be called "the Dee." The patients were accompanied by five graduate nurses: Maude Edwards, Beda Nelson Woodbury, Winifred Howard Jarvis, Alice Manning, and Mary Hornsby. Maude Edwards was named the Dee's first superintendent of nurses. By the time the hospital's board of trustees convened on January 19, 1911, 77 patients had been admitted. Twenty-eight were discharged, and five deaths had occurred. The Dee's rates were initially $3 a day for a private room and $2 per day for a bed in a ward. Railroad patients were charged $1.50 per day with no charge for the operating room. Maternity cases were $25 for 14 days. Nurses worked a 12-hour day with a half-day off per week when permitted by the patient load.

The average daily revenue per patient by July was $2.63, which was only 2 cents above the daily cost per patient. The first year's statistics showed 895 patients were served and 481 operations performed. There were only five births, primarily because births at the time commonly occurred at home. To encourage lower mortality rates and improved care and training opportunities for student nurses, Annie personally paid the hospital fee of $25 for 14 days to any woman who would have her baby in the hospital, as reported in *A Tradition of Caring*.

I, with my mother, Mary Elizabeth "Betty" Dee Shaw, witnessed the laying of the cornerstone of the first Dee Hospital. Very soon thereafter, I became the youngest patient for surgery (so I was told) when I had the removal of my appendix done by Dr. Joyce and Dr. Ezra Rich.

— Elizabeth Shaw Stewart
First granddaughter of
Thomas and Annie Dee

Organizations contributing to the Dee Memorial Hospital

- EASTERN STAR LODGE: $200
- WEBER CLUB: $500
- MARTHA SOCIETY: FURNISHINGS FOR AN EIGHT-BED ROOM ON THE WOMEN'S FLOOR
- AMALGAMATED SUGAR COMPANY: $500
- WEBER STAKE RELIEF SOCIETY: FURNISHINGS FOR A SIX-BED WARD
- BROTHERHOOD OF RAILROAD TRAINMEN
- G.W. LARKIN
- W.H. WATTIS
- H.H. ROLAPP
- MISS KATHRYN JOYCE
- MRS. JOHN SCOWCROFT
- S.J. BURT BROTHERS
- W.H. WRIGHT AND SON
- BECKER BREWING COMPANY
- OGDEN STAKE RELIEF SOCIETY
- FATHER P. M. CUSHNAHAN
- MISS ROSABELLE DEE
- OGDEN FURNITURE AND CARPET CO.
- MASONIC LODGE

Facing: Main entrance on Harrison Boulevard of the Thomas D. Dee Memorial Hospital, in Ogden, Utah.

Thomas D. Dee Memorial Hospital Dedication Program

———————

December 29, 1910 • 3 p.m. to 8 p.m.
Reverend Father Patrick M. Cushnahan, Pastor of St. Joseph's Catholic Church Presiding

Invocation: Bishop James Taylor
Address: Judge Henry R. Rolapp
Formal Tendering of the Hospital to the Public: Mrs. Thomas D. Dee
Responses of Acceptance: Mayor William Glasmann, O.B. Madsen (Chairman, Weber County Commission), A.R. Heywood (President, Weber Club), Dr. E.C. Rich (Ogden Medical Society)
The Hospital and the Community: LDS Apostle David O. McKay
Honoring Thomas D. Dee: Dr. A.S. Condon
Benediction: the Rev. J.E. Carver

Members of the Thomas D. Dee Memorial Hospital's Board of Trustees at its opening in 1910 included:

———————

ANNIE TAYLOR DEE, *President*

FATHER P.M. CUSHNAHAN, *Vice President*

JOHN S. LEWIS, *Vice President*

JOHN WATSON, *Treasurer*

MAUDE DEE PORTER, *Secretary*

JUDGE HENRY H. ROLAPP, FRED J. KIESEL, R.B. PORTER

WILLIAM GLASMANN, *Mayor of Ogden*

DR. ROBERT S. JOYCE, *Chief of Staff*

DR. E.M. CONROY

THE DEE BECAME KNOWN AS AN EXCELLENT HOSPITAL

With a state-of-the-art building, skilled and committed physicians and nurses, and an involved board backed by the Dee family, the hospital soon gained an excellent reputation. Dr. R.C. McCloskey from Chicago was employed as the hospital's first internist in November 1911. His salary was $35 a month plus railroad fare from Chicago. By 1913, the first class of trained nurses from the Dee Memorial Hospital School of Nursing began their employment. Ogden's first X-ray machine, a gift from Drs. Rich and Osgood, arrived in 1913. An X-ray of a hip joint required a 10-minute exposure; it takes just seconds today with modern technology.

Top: Patient room at the Dee Memorial Hospital furnished by Ogden community members.

Bottom: Lab at the Dee Memorial Hospital.

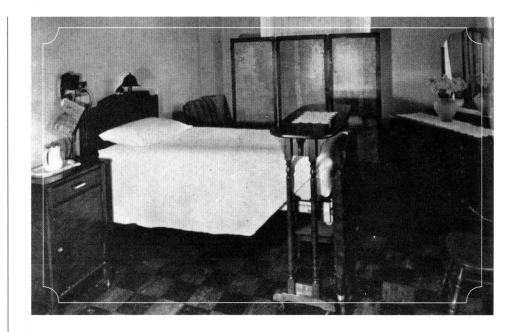

Thirty-four physicians were listed as members of the staff at the hospital's opening in 1910:

Dr. Robert S. Joyce,
Chief of Staff
Dr. G.W. Baker
Dr. W.J. Browning
Dr. F.C. Clark
Dr. A.S. Condon
Dr. E.M. Conroy
Dr. C.E. Coulter
Dr. L.H. Cranshaw
Dr. George A. Dickson
Dr. T.C. Doran
Dr. John Driver
Dr. E.R. Dumke
Dr. H.B. Forbes
Dr. W.G. Freiday
Dr. J.S. Gordon
Dr. G.W. Green
Dr. C.C. Hetzel

Dr. Paul Ingebretson
Dr. E.P. Mills
Dr. J.R. Morrell
Dr. C.K. MacMurdy
Dr. O.S. Osgood
Dr. J.W. Pidcock
Dr. H.J. Powers
Dr. L.R. Pugmire
Dr. Ezra C. Rich
Dr. E.I. Rich
Dr. Alice M. Ridge
Dr. D.F. Ries
Dr. A.A. Robinson
Dr. E.H. Smith
Dr. C.E. Wardleigh
Dr. W.E. Whalen
Dr. E.M. Worrell

(Some records also refer to 32 physicians initially on staff.)

A "Dee Hospital first" occurred on February 19, 1913, when Dr. Ezra Rich performed Ogden's first blood transfusion using direct gravity flow between brothers, one of whom was injured in a sawmill accident near Malad, Idaho. The injured patient recovered, even though blood typing and cross matching was unknown at that time.

From *A Tradition of Caring*

Left: The initials on this doctor's bag, C.C.H., possibly belonged to Dr. C.C. Hetzel, listed among the Dee's original physicians.

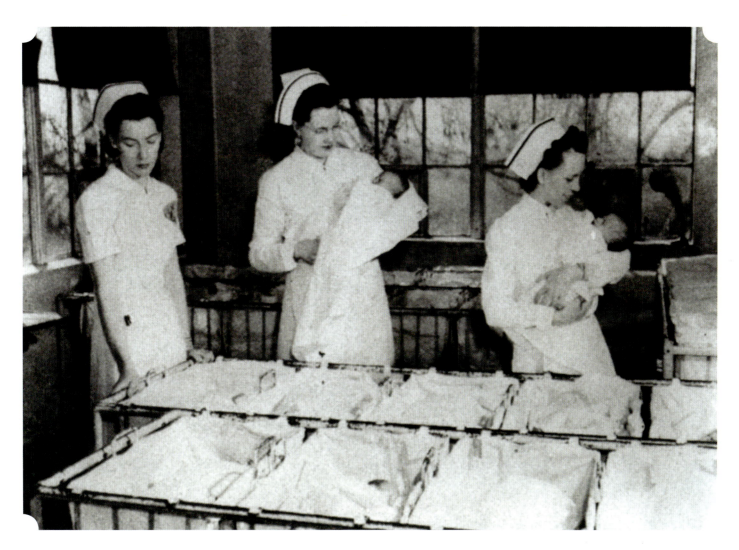

Above and right:
Dee nurses care for newborns. In the early years, Annie Taylor Dee personally paid the hospital fee of $25 for 14 days to any woman who would give birth in the hospital.

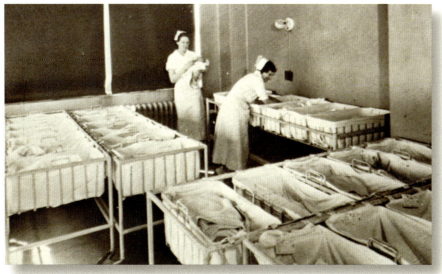

Left: The fully equipped "modern" Dee Hospital laundry.

Below, right: Dee Hospital operating table and room, circa 1930.

Inset: Medical instruments of the day.

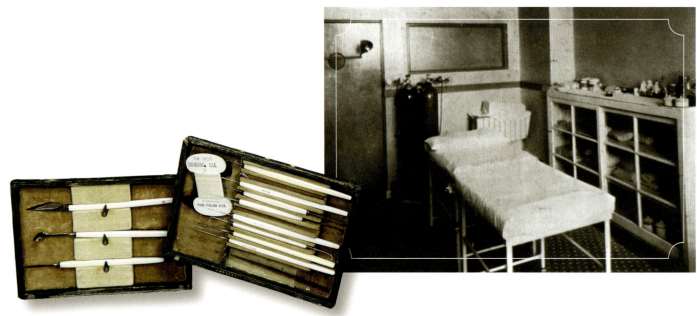

FINANCIAL CRISIS

Although the Dee's reputation and patient load continued to grow, the Thomas D. Dee Company had borne the hospital's entire administrative and financial burden, and operating expenses began to outstrip available resources, according to *A Tradition of Caring*. By 1914, Annie and her family concluded they could no longer sustain the operating deficit. The hospital owed $6,000, and Vice President John S. Lewis was authorized by the board of trustees to negotiate a loan. Later, the trustees concluded, "It is apparent at the present time that the hospital cannot continue to operate unless a maintenance fund can be created to meet the expense of improvements and extensions." All concerned were disheartened. On October 23, 1914, a resolution was passed to discontinue operations. The board thanked the Thomas D. Dee Company members for their "generous effort to establish a hospital in this city, and for their continued financial support given to it during its operation." Behind the scenes, however, efforts to save the hospital were under way. The Weber Club proposed active management by a committee of 50 leading citizens to raise $5,000 and develop a plan for obtaining another $20,000 for new equipment and improvements.

"Then the time came when Mother had to take money out of her savings to run the hospital," Maude reflected later. "I can remember

Ogden, Utah, Feby. 8,1915.

Mrs. Annie T. Dee,

City.

Dear Sister Dee:-

Your letter of the 5th inst. to President Joseph F. Smith and Counselors, containing your answer to the proposition made by the three Stake Presidencies as presented by the Committee of the Council of Twelve, also the Treasurer's report of the Hospital for January, came to hand to-day.

I shall present it to the Committee to-morrow, with the view of making definite recommendations to the Presidency and Council of Twelve next Thursday.

Respectfully yours,

David O. McKay.

Above: A letter from Elder David O. McKay, a member of the LDS Church's Quorum of Twelve Apostles, who acted as Dee family liaison to affect a transfer of the Thomas D. Dee Memorial Hospital to Church ownership in 1915. When a new hospital opened in 1969, it was initially named the David O. McKay Hospital.

how depressed we were that the hospital was going to fail. We didn't want that to happen, so Mother decided to talk to our friend, Elder David O. McKay." Annie made a personal appeal to the Weber County native and apostle in the LDS Church.

As reported in detail in *A Tradition of Caring*, an interview was arranged with the LDS Church's First Presidency. Maude remembers President Anthon H. Lund, Second Counselor in the First Presidency, saying, "It is my opinion that the best work we can do is to take care of people who are sick and dependent at a time when they are in trouble." Father Patrick M. Cushnahan, the Catholic priest who had been a member of the board since its inception, made a verbal offer for his church to assume the hospital's expenses. Other efforts to save the hospital were initiated by the presidencies of the Ogden, Weber, and North Weber LDS stakes, who proposed forming the Weber Corporation of the LDS Church to own and operate the Dee. Their proposal eventually merged with the discussions between the Dee family and the LDS First Presidency in Salt Lake City. At the hospital's annual meeting in 1915, it was announced that the LDS Church had taken over operation of the hospital, and Annie Taylor Dee was appointed Honorary Matron. She accepted and presented the hospital with a check for $5,140. The minutes also record that the First Presidency authorized an appropriation for improvements including a storeroom, refitted X-ray and hydrotherapy rooms, new equipment, and linen. Out of respect to the Dee family and as a tribute to their tremendous

efforts, the hospital's new articles of incorporation stipulated that a member of the Dee family would always have representation on the board of trustees; the agreement continues to this day.

Right: This letter, dated February 11, 1915, signaled that the Dee would remain viable and operated by the LDS Church. This was the second hospital owned and operated by the Church, after LDS Hospital in Salt Lake City. The transfer of the Dee to the Church is considered the beginning of the Church's multi-hospital system.

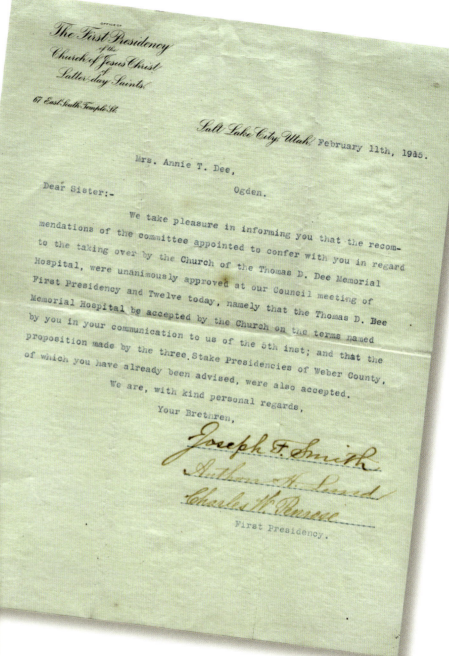

Facing: In celebration of Hospital Day in 1923, all babies born at the hospital the previous year and their mothers gathered to have their picture taken.

Left: After ownership transfer of the hospital to the LDS Church, Annie Dee continued to advocate for affordable, accessible healthcare. In 1923, the Dee children honored their parents by establishing a Memorial Room as a place of solace for patients and families. This is a 1918 photograph of Annie at age 66. She died on April 10, 1934, at age 82.

Change and Growth

With the Dee on more sound financial footing because of LDS Church involvement and under the able leadership of outstanding administrators and medical staff, the hospital was poised for unprecedented growth and improvements in patient care. Under the leadership of R.C. Lundy, 1910–15; O.J. Stillwell, 1915–16; Wilfred W. Rawson, 1917–33; Howard Jenkins, 1933–41; Lawrence Evans, 1941–45; and Kenneth E. Knapp, 1951–72, hospital assets grew from $110,000 in 1910 to $4,301,627 in 1968. During that period, 11 major additions were made to the hospital, along with hundreds of smaller internal remodeling projects. LeGrand Richards, Presiding Bishop of the LDS Church and chairman of the hospital's board of trustees from 1938 to 1958, set the hospital on a new course of management when he recruited Kenneth Knapp, an executive for United Airlines. Knapp was enrolled in hospital administration classes at Northwestern University and served internships at hospitals in Chicago, Detroit, and Cleveland. He was appointed administrator of the Dee in April 1951. Knapp found the Dee in a precarious financial situation and immediately consolidated departments, reduced personnel, and closed patient units, according to *A Tradition of Caring*. Community service organizations were invited to lease space in the building to bolster hospital income.

Knapp also led the move with the medical staff to formulate a constitution and bylaws that set standards for expanded residency and intern training. That helped the hospital apply for accreditation by the Joint Commission on Accreditation of Hospitals, making the Dee the first hospital in Utah to achieve the designation.

Under Knapp's leadership, the hospital began an era of transformation. In August 1951, just four months after joining the hospital, Knapp began planning a floor-by-floor renovation of the Dee. He said he set aside half of every dollar that exceeded expenses, and when enough money was accumulated, he would have a change made – a bathroom or other convenience that "made hospitalization at the Dee a little more attractive and comfortable for the patient."

The polio epidemic of 1951 was crippling – and killing – an astounding number of people, so Knapp added a polio ward, complete with an iron lung. Nurses willing to work in this area – endangering their health and their very lives – were recruited to work with the polio patients.

Evolving building and fire codes prompted more extensive changes to the hospital, but Knapp was determined to keep the hospital within its income. "It was not unusual for management people to wear many hats and even come back in the evening to wield a paintbrush," he said.

As reported in *A Tradition of Caring*, over 10 years and with a $523,000 modernization plan, Knapp instituted the first psychiatric division in a Utah general hospital. Physical Therapy, Anesthesia, Continuing Education, Childbirth Education, and Personnel departments took root under his watch. An Outpatient department was organized, a new Neuropsychiatric division was created, Radiology was expanded and provided new equipment, and the maternity area was upgraded and a new nursery was added.

New Pediatric and Orthopedic areas, surgical suites, and a post-operative recovery room were completed, as were new administrative offices, a staff lounge, and a library. The hospital's waiting areas were redecorated, and the elevators were modernized.

Hospital patients benefited from the addition of piped oxygen and a unique "blood assurance" program begun to ensure a continuing supply of donated blood in the hospital blood bank. An intercom system was installed that allowed patients to communicate with workers at nurses' stations. A Nuclear Medicine department and a clinical laboratory were added. A Social Services department was organized, and in 1953, Knapp opened a daycare nursery for hospital employees' children. Additions included a laundry and kitchen.

During all of these changes, those in the healthcare industry began to realize that nurses needed more scientific and medical knowledge, so in 1955, what was then Weber College in Ogden took over nurses' education from the hospital. However, the hospital remained essential to nurses' training – it provided clinical experience at patients' bedside. The Dee School of Nursing had graduated more than 700 nurses in its 42 years.

In 1959, the Dee opened one of the region's first intensive care units for the care of the critically ill and gravely injured.

In 1963, the Annie T. Dee Foundation underwrote the operation of a new home care program, the only hospital-based home healthcare program in Utah until the federal government sponsored a similar program near Richfield, Utah, in the 1970s.

The Dee's 24-hour emergency care began in 1966, thanks to three physicians willing to rotate shifts to ensure constant coverage. The hospital also tested the Multi-Level Care concept, with patients placed according to the amount of care their condition demanded.

I first worked as a unit clerk in the Emergency Room at the old Dee as a teenager in the '60s. It really was just a room then. Ambulance service was provided by the local taxi service. The company did have an actual ambulance; it was a modified funeral hearse with big tail fins. When an emergency call came in (from the Dee or a physician), the taxi dispatcher radioed one of their drivers to return to the garage, get the "ambulance" and go to the scene.

The Dee was only the second hospital in the United States to have physicians totally dedicated to the ER, 24 hours a day. This was long before Emergency Medicine was a distinct specialty.

— Kayleen Paul, RN, Director of Critical Care,
Emergency and Trauma Services

HARD DECISIONS TO MAKE

As the 1960s approached and upgrades and additions to the hospital were being made, even larger upgrades and additions seemed to be around the corner. The hospital's Board of Trustees began asking whether it would be better to continue in those costly endeavors or just build a whole new hospital that would meet evolving needs. The Dee was almost 50 years old when a thorough examination of the physical structure was conducted. Also at that time, about 1957, a nationally recognized consultant was hired to review the community's future healthcare needs. After reviewing both studies, the board, with the approval of the LDS Church's Presiding Bishopric (tasked with management of temporal assets and operations for the entire Church), recommended that a new hospital be built.

Presiding Bishop Thorpe B. Isaacson had noted, "Operation of the Dee has become difficult and burdensome. It is no longer considered feasible to try to bring the old building up to acceptable standards."

A 27-acre parcel at 3939 Harrison Boulevard – just a tad more than two miles south of the Dee – was acquired and, in 1958, it was announced that a new $5 million hospital would be built, according to *A Tradition of Caring*.

Knapp, who had championed the Dee's continued growth and upgrades since his April 1951 hiring, was now tapped to lead a committee tasked with raising $1.6 million from the community. However, after a lackluster response from area residents, planning for the new hospital was suspended and the Dee continued to grow and improve to accommodate patients' needs. Two years after the initial fundraising attempt, efforts resumed in full force. In July 1960, the Dee medical staff met with Knapp and recruited local businessman Rulon White to lead the charge in raising the $1.6 million. By 1962, enough had been raised that LDS Presiding Bishop John H. Vandenberg announced that Ogden's Keith W. Wilcox would design the new hospital in honor of LDS Church President David O. McKay, who had been so instrumental in keeping the Dee going under the LDS Church's care in 1915. Lawrence T. Dee expressed his family's support, saying it was

Our committee was given an assignment of $800,000, but before I could get the committee organized, our assignment had been raised to $1 million on account of increased costs. We set a goal for the committee of $1.6 million. During the life of the committee, over $1.8 million was pledged or paid in cash. Pledges and cash payments went from a few dollars to an individual pledge of $175,000. The David O. McKay Hospital was built and paid for and dedicated July 9, 1969. We were released and thanked for our services.

—J.R. Bachman, chairman of the David O. McKay
Hospital Building Fund Committee

Above: J.R. Bachman, a retired executive of the Amalgamated Sugar Company in Ogden, Utah, kept a journal *(right and inset)* documenting his efforts to help raise funds for the new hospital.

— 42 —

She is also crippled and walks with a cane. She can do no cooking, sewing or fancy work and does only minor household tasks. She reads a lot or just sits. We have visitors from family and friends and also try to go out each day in the auto.

I was concerned about retirement but what I would do after but I need not have been as various things came along.

In September of 1961 I was called by The First Presidency of the L.D.S. Church to be the Chairman of the David O. McKay Hospital Building Fund Committee. The church had the Dee Hospital in Ogden but had decided to build a new hospital. This hospital was to be financed by the Church and by contributions from Wards and Stakes, business men and individuals in the area to be served which was Box Elder, North Davis, Morgan and Weber Counties. Our committee was given an assignment of $800,000⁰⁰, but before I could get the committee organized our assignment had been raised to $1,000,000⁰⁰ on account of increased costs.

The Church had agreed to hire an office man and give us office space in

NO PARKING

"fitting and proper" for the hospital to so memorialize the community and church leader.

Funds raised for the hospital reached $450,000 by 1965, thanks to contributions by physicians and the Volunteer Auxiliary, which was established in 1954. These contributions were augmented by significant memorial gifts from Dee Family Charitable Trusts and Foundations. On April 20, 1966, the LDS Church First Presidency authorized construction of the David O. McKay Hospital. The cost was now estimated to exceed $9.9 million, as reported in *A Tradition of Caring*.

THE END OF THE ORIGINAL DEE

As construction of McKay began, thoughts turned to the future of the existing Dee facilities. Hospital administrators finalized an agreement with the state to take over care of tuberculosis patients housed in the State Sanitarium on North Harrison Boulevard. The Dee was to be a rehabilitation center and convalescent hospital after patients were transferred to the David O. McKay Hospital. However, it soon became apparent that the plan was financially unsound because of aging facilities and infrastructure.

By June 1968, it was decided the Dee could best serve the community as a new hospital adjacent to the McKay building going up at 3939 Harrison Boulevard. This plan would fulfill the LDS Church's commitment to the Dee family in 1916 that "there will always be a Dee Hospital in Ogden." By December, the First Presidency announced $2.1 million would be available for the building of the new Dee, and a Medical Staff committee was formed to help in its planning. In 1968, the McKay-Dee Hospital Foundation formed to support fundraising efforts.

The old Dee's last remaining ward, the tuberculosis ward, closed June 30, 1970. The tuberculosis patients were transferred to the Weber County Hospital – but not before a poignant farewell party for patients and staff. Memories of

the building's 60-year legacy were celebrated, and excitement and optimism built as plans to move into the new facility began to take shape.

Facing: By the 1960s, the Dee was showing its age in spite of several expansions and many improvements.

Previous pages: The Dee's emergency entrance on the corner of 24th Street and Harrison in Ogden. Emergency Room coverage 24 hours a day by physicians began in 1966.

Above: During the demolition of the original Dee Memorial Hospital, the cornerstone box was removed. In this photo, Lawrence T. Dee and his son Thomas D. Dee II watch as engineer Frank Southwick pries open the box. Contents deposited in 1909 included Dee family memorabilia and photographs, a panoramic postcard of Ogden, and copies of three newspapers from the cornerstone ceremony date of September 27, 1910.

After the move to the new hospital campus a little more than two miles to the south in 1969, the Dee continued briefly as a convalescent hospital before being demolished in November 1972. The site stood empty for a few years before it was donated by the Dee family to the city of Ogden to become a public park. The site is now Dee Memorial Park.

From Hospital to Park

Two years later, in November 1972, the old Dee facility was demolished. The site stood empty for a few years, and then neighbors approached the Dee family, suggesting the grounds be made a public park. The Dee family embraced that idea and donated the land to the city of Ogden.

Dee Memorial Park was dedicated in 1980. It features green space and pavilions for gatherings, as well as a monument to the site's history. Hospital employees commemorated 60 years of service to the sick and injured with the donation of a plaque on a large stone monument (seen at right). Another plaque, set to its right, was donated by the Dee Hospital Alumni Nurses Association in 1981. It honors the 720 graduates of the Thomas D. Dee Memorial Hospital School of Nursing between 1911 and 1951. Special note is made of nurses who served in the armed forces during World War I and World War II, as well as those who provided special care during epidemics and other emergencies.

One hundred years after the Dee opened on the site to serve residents in a health capacity, the site is still serving area residents as a park and welcome green space in a community that has expanded, grown more dense and embraced the outdoor recreation opportunities the Wasatch Front offers.

The Dee family gave the land to the city of Ogden, and in 1980, Ogden City Corporation held a dedication ceremony for the Dee Memorial Park. Contributions by local residents, as well as civic and professional groups, developed the donated site into the park. "This park will be put to good use for the children and people of the community," Mrs. Marama Hansen, president of the Dee Nurses Alumni Association, said at the dedication of the nurses' plaque.

Left: This *Ogden Standard-Examiner* photo shows the grandson of Thomas Duncombe Dee, Thomas D. Dee II, preparing to cut the ribbon at the ceremony dedicating Dee Memorial Park at 24th Street and Harrison Boulevard in 1980.

Breaking Ground for the New McKay

The much-anticipated ground-breaking for the new David O. McKay Hospital took place on a rain-soaked field on April 23, 1966, nine years after the decision to replace the Dee. LDS Church President David O. McKay, the person whose name would grace the new facility, threw a switch triggering a dynamite explosion, which signaled the start of construction.

Though the event began under overcast skies, they eventually cleared. Referring to the hospital's opening, which wouldn't be for a few years, McKay, who was now in his ninth decade, said, "I don't know where you'll be, but I'm not going anyplace, and I plan to be here!"

Above: David O. McKay, president of The Church of Jesus Christ of Latter-day Saints, appears to be enjoying himself as he flips a switch to trigger a dynamite explosion, kicking off construction for his namesake hospital on April 23, 1966.

Right: The ungraded and unpaved parking lot at the McKay Hospital would soon fill with the cars of patients, physicians, visitors, clergy, and staff.

Below: David O. McKay Hospital under construction circa 1968. McKay Hospital's distinctive silhouette dramatically altered Ogden's East Bench skyline.

On May 16, 1969, LDS President David O. McKay paid a 40-minute surprise visit to the nearly completed McKay Hospital. After a wheelchair tour, he told hospital architect Keith W. Wilcox: "I am deeply moved that this great hospital should become a tribute to me; no man could ask for a greater honor. Visiting it is one of the very impressive experiences of my life. I am so grateful to all who made it possible."

Engineers had been in the new building six months before the new David O. McKay Hospital opened in order to become completely familiar with the entire 334,210-square-foot complex. Twenty employees were required in the McKay-Dee Engineering Department to ensure a well-run hospital.

The new David O. McKay Hospital's 27-acre campus at 3939 Harrison Boulevard took shape rapidly as crews worked to meet the completion deadlines.

A New Hospital for a New Time

→ 1969 *to* 2002 ←

DESPITE CONSTRUCTION DELAYS and inclement weather, as reported in *A Tradition of Caring*, the new David D. McKay Hospital was formally dedicated July 9, 1969. Nearly 1,500 people, representing a cross section of community, religious, and government leaders, gathered for the event celebrating the opening of a new hospital that would offer hope, comfort, and healing to thousands who would pass through its doors over the next three decades.

True to his word, LDS Church President David O. McKay – now 95 years old – attended, but because of his increasingly frail health, he remained in his car. Ogden Mayor and dentist Bart Wolthius told those gathered for the ceremony that Ogden was proud to have a hospital named "for one of Utah's most honored sons."

In celebration of the new hospital and the services it would provide to those suffering from various ailments and injuries, Wolthius went on to say, "Good health animates all the enjoyments of life, and without it, all enjoyments fade."

On July 9, 1969, nearly 1,500 enthusiastic participants, representing a cross section of community, religious, and government leaders, gathered for dedication ceremonies of the new David O. McKay Hospital. Just a little more than two miles south of 59-year old Thomas D. Dee Memorial Hospital, the new hospital offered hope, comfort, and healing to thousands who would pass through its doors over the next three decades.

Top: Attendees at the dedication of the David O. McKay Hospital included, *from left:* Mr. and Mrs. Joel Ricks, Mrs. Scott B. Price, Mr. and Mrs. Lawrence T. Dee, Mr. Scott Price, the Rev. Emmett Dosier, and Mrs. LaVern Parmley, LDS Church General Primary President.

Left: David Lawrence McKay represented his father, LDS Church President David O. McKay, at the dedication ceremony.

Inset: John H. Vandenberg, Presiding LDS Bishop and president of the board of trustees, gave laudatory remarks at the dedication program of the new McKay Hospital.

Above: The completed and operational McKay-Dee Hospital Center at 3939 Harrison Boulevard as it appeared in the 1970s.

Inset: Administrator Kenneth Knapp presented LDS Church President David O. McKay with this key to the hospital's front door and promised: "These doors will never be locked again."

That sentiment was reinforced by McKay's son, David Lawrence McKay, when he said, "The hospital has been completed to relieve suffering and pain and to restore new hope and life to thousands who will pass through its doors in years to come."

Other speakers during the 35-minute dedication ceremony included LDS Church Presiding Bishop John H. Vandenberg; McKay Administrator Kenneth Knapp; and Dr. Joe Amano, president of the hospital's medical staff.

"This hospital is a dream come true as the result of the devotion of many people," Vandenberg told the crowd. "It stands as a monument to man's willingness to serve mankind without thought of profit."

Knapp called the new David O. McKay Hospital a "culmination of a need which became a force and now is a reality to serve the residents of Ogden."

To reinforce the hospital's focus of providing healthcare whenever needed, Knapp presented the LDS Church president with the key to the hospital's front door, promising "these doors will never be locked again."

MOVING TO THE NEW McKAY

Three days after McKay's dedication ceremony, 154 patients were transferred from the Dee to the McKay. The smooth transition on July 12, 1969, took only two hours and 40 minutes, thanks to careful planning and coordination.

As patients and personnel settled in, three graduate physicians from the University of Utah began surgery residencies at the McKay. The new program meant surgery residents spent a three- to six-month rotation at the McKay, working with local surgeons holding University of Utah faculty appointments.

The David O. McKay Hospital thrived in its first year. In 1970, the hospital reported the following services:

- 17,000 patients admitted
- 111,600 days of patient care
- 62,000 outpatients treated
- 20,500 emergencies handled
- 404,700 lab procedures performed
- 3,200 babies delivered
- 28,150 X-ray procedures performed
- 255,500 prescriptions provided
- 55,700 or more volunteer hours donated
- 350,000 meals served
- 1,006,000 pounds of linen laundered

Additionally, the hospital contributed to the local economy by purchasing $2.5 million in supplies and paying more than $5 million in wages and benefits to 920 full- and part-time employees.

On January 18, 1970, the entire hospital joined the community and members of The Church of Jesus Christ of Latter-day Saints in mourning when LDS Church President David O. McKay passed away at age 96. He had been instrumental in the survival of the Thomas D. Dee Memorial Hospital back in 1914-15 and had been so revered that the Ogden hospital was named to honor him.

LDS Church Presiding Bishop John H. Vandenberg said, "He was a friend to all mankind, and we are proud to serve in the institution that bears his name."

On February 5, 1971, a stained-mahogany David O. McKay memorial mural was unveiled following a ceremony in the hospital auditorium. Commissioned through a $10,000 grant from Norman B. and Melba Bingham, of Ogden, artist Lorin G. Folland Jr. worked two years to complete a tribute to the late LDS Church President's Love of Home, Love of Learning, Love of God, Love of Neighbor, and Love of Country, each illustrated on a separate panel nine feet high and titled on a plaque lettered in gold.

Three days after the new hospital was dedicated, a logistical undertaking months in the planning began. At 7:45 a.m. on July 12, 1969, the hospital's Clinical Director of Medicine, Joanne Marriott, RN, dispatched the car carrying the first patients — two infants and their mothers — from the 59-year-old Dee Hospital to the new David O. McKay Hospital. These baby boys, born just three days before, and their mothers, Mrs. Robert F. Moore and Mrs. David Tribe, were the first patients moved from the Dee to the McKay. The move of the 129 adults and children, plus 25 infants, is believed to have been the largest in Utah medical history at the time. A mini-bus, loaned by the Golden Hours Center in Ogden, ambulance crews from Hill Air Force Base, Moss Ambulance, and transports from Home Care Service assisted. The last two patients, one in traction and the other in a "Stryker" bed, were moved in a Redman moving van and entered the McKay Hospital through the loading dock instead of the front door. The plan worked so smoothly that the patient move was completed at 10:50 a.m., in three hours and five minutes — a good hour ahead of the most optimistic estimate.

What a day! All new beds, linens, and equipment, O^2 (oxygen) in all rooms, bathrooms in each room and (in the) wards, tube system instead of elevators, and a clean holding (place) on the unit for all of our supplies.

— Delpha Greaves Allen, nurse (class of 1948), who made the transition from the Dee with her patients

Planning for a Dee Wing at McKay

Back when plans for the new David O. McKay Hospital were announced, the old Dee had been expected to find new life as a rehabilitation facility. Many Dee services were to be shared with the McKay: dietary, engineering, laboratory, surgical, and business and medical records. However, it became apparent that the old structure was in no shape to fulfill even that limited mission. With the support of the Dee family, it was announced that a new hospital bearing the Dee family's name was to be built adjacent to the McKay Hospital at 3939 Harrison Boulevard.

On January 15, 1970, three days before the death of LDS Church President David O. McKay, bids were

The stained-mahogany David O. McKay memorial mural was unveiled on February 5, 1971, following a program in the hospital auditorium. Artist Lorin G. Folland Jr. worked two years to complete the mural commissioned through a $10,000 grant from Norman B. and Melba Bingham, of Ogden. Folland expressed his inspiration for the mural: The late LDS president's Love of Home, Love of Learning, Love of God, Love of Neighbor, and Love of Country illustrated on five separate panels each nine feet high. Beneath each panel was a plaque bearing its title lettered in gold.

opened for the new Thomas D. Dee Memorial Hospital, but they came in considerably higher than expected. The architect was asked to make modifications, but Lawrence T. Dee and his son, Thomas D. Dee II, who were at the bid opening, decided they were unwilling to compromise standards and expectations. They called family members and collected a quarter of a million dollars so they could have the hospital they wanted and a facility that would best honor Thomas Duncombe Dee.

The announced estimated cost for the new Dee, including furnishings, was $2.3 million, and Culp Construction Co., of Salt Lake City, began construction on April 29, 1970, after a ground-breaking ceremony earlier that day. At the event, Ogden Mayor Bart Wolthius summed up the widespread enthusiasm by issuing a proclamation declaring April 29, 1970, "Dee Day."

"In fact, when I review the contributions made by this marvelous family, I wonder why we don't have Dee Day every year," he said. The Dee family contributed $150,000 toward the project from the Annie T. Dee Foundation and $100,000 from the Elizabeth Dee Shaw Foundation. Yet another contribution from the Dee family came in June 1970 when Joseph F. Barker gave $25,000 to be used to memorialize his wife, the late Rosabelle Dee Barker.

P R O C L A M A T I O N

PROCLAMATION DECLARING WEDNESDAY, APRIL 29, 1970, "DEE DAY."

WHEREAS, Mrs. Annie Taylor Dee and her children -- Maude Dee Porter, Elizabeth Dee Shaw, Margaret Dee Higginbotham, Edith Dee Green, Florence Dee Barker, Rosabelle Dee Barker, Lawrence T. Dee -- founded the Thomas D. Dee Memorial Hospital in memory of their husband and father, which opened on December 29, 1910; and

WHEREAS, the Dee family has rendered the entire Ogden area a needed and valued service through their continuing support of the Thomas D. Dee Memorial Hospital during the ensuing 60 years; and

WHEREAS, the administration of the McKay-Dee Hospital Center has deemed it suitable to schedule construction ceremonies for the start of a new Hospital at 3939 Harrison Boulevard to bear the Dee family name;

NOW, THEREFORE, I, Bart Wolthuis, Mayor of Ogden City, on behalf of the residents of this city and the people in the area who in the past were served by the Thomas D. Dee Memorial Hospital and who in the future will be served by the new facility which will bear the same name, express our sincere and heartfelt appreciation to the Thomas D. Dee family for their long and ardent support with their time and money of this vital community hospital.

I further declare Wednesday, April 29, 1970, as "DEE DAY."

DATED this 23rd day of April, 1970.

_____
MAYOR

ATTEST:

_____
CITY RECORDER

In Memory of President McKay

At LDS President David O. McKay's death at age 96 on January 18, 1970, the entire McKay-Dee Hospital family mourned him. According to Bishop Vandenberg, "He was a friend to all mankind, and we are proud to serve in the institution that bears his name."

Above: Lawrence T. Dee talks about the site of the new Thomas D. Dee Memorial Hospital with his sister, Maude Dee Porter, circa 1970.

Left: Thomas (Tim) Dee III and brother David, great-grandsons of Thomas D. Dee, break ground for the new Dee Hospital on April 29, 1970. The Dee family's gift of $250,000 made possible the completion of the fifth floor, which would have been left in a "roughed-in" state until funds could be found.

The Birth of the McKay-Dee Name

The Dee Hospital was dedicated and opened on November 10, 1971, 29 months after the McKay Hospital opened. It was also the 127th anniversary of the day Thomas Duncombe Dee was born.

With the opening of the new Dee wing adjacent to McKay, the hospital campus became known as the McKay-Dee Hospital Center.

Formation of Health Services Corporation

While the Dee wing was being built adjacent to the McKay Hospital, the LDS Church announced the formation of Health Services Corporation, which effectively ended the era of the LDS Church hospital system begun in 1915. Even though all 15 hospitals, including the McKay-Dee Hospital Center, were still Church-owned and -operated, the individual hospital boards now came under control of a central HSC board in May 1970. As part of the reorganization, HSC named Kenneth E. Knapp as associate commissioner. He had served for 21 years as administrator of the Dee and McKay hospitals. Kenneth C. Johnson, who was transferred from Primary Children's Medical Center in Salt Lake City, replaced him. The Governing Board of McKay-Dee reorganized into a nine-member board with Lawrence T. Dee as vice chairman.

McKay-Dee Strives to Continually Improve

As contributions flowed in, a special procedures operating room was endowed by Mrs. Clark Rich and her daughters in memory of Clark L. Rich, MD. A $25,000 contribution from Mrs. Margaret Higgenbotham resulted in a new dining room named in her honor in the Dee wing.

In 1971, a helistop underwritten by the J. Clyde Buehler family opened near the Emergency Room, and the first open-heart surgery in the Ogden area was performed at McKay. Heart-lung bypass pumps and three qualified thoracic surgeons on staff meant patients no longer had to undergo life-saving surgery far from home in Salt Lake City.

Johnson began a $250,000 remodeling project on the McKay's second floor in early 1973, just three and a half years after the hospital's opening. The addition included two more private labor rooms, bringing the total to 10. Each was enlarged to accommodate fetal heart-monitoring equipment. The Intensive Care Nursery was expanded to include eight incubators and an adjacent high-risk delivery room. A recovery area for new mothers was added in the postpartum wing, along with a father's waiting room.

In celebration of her 90th birthday on May 3, 1973, Edith Dee Mack Green gave $250,000 to build an auditorium and learning center on the B level of the McKay. Not more than six months later, her sons, Wade and Harold Mack, and her granddaughter, Dee Ann Nye, memorialized the Physical Therapy department to their brother and father, respectively, Glenn Dee Mack. Nye also memorialized the Speech Pathology area to her son, Scott, who had been killed in a climbing accident.

The next year, the area's first physiatrist, John M. Bender, MD, joined the hospital-based staff to direct a new physical medicine and rehabilitation program based in the Dee wing.

Occasionally, giant helicopters from nearby Hill Air Force Base made stops at McKay-Dee in the '70s and '80s. Lois Chard, RN, Administrative Nursing Coordinator, recalled in a 1976 employee newsletter that she heard the voice of an air-traffic controller at Hill Air Force Base informing her he had dispatched a helicopter to a remote area of Box Elder County on the shores of Great Salt Lake. A small plane had gone

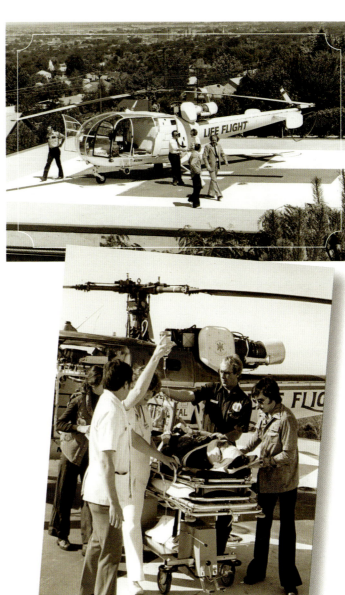

Above: Through a generous gift of J. Clyde and Eleanor Buehler, of Ogden, the helistop at McKay-Dee Hospital began operations in July 1971. Mr. and Mrs. Buehler flew from the Ogden Airport aboard a Key Airlines "chopper" and were the first to touch down at the new facility. Mr. Buehler said, "Our family felt that a helicopter landing pad located right at the door of this very fine emergency room would be an additional life-saving feature we could all be proud of." Before today's well-known Life Flight "choppers," AirMed, based at LDS Hospital in Salt Lake City, provided service to McKay-Dee.

Above: Ready availability of helicopters improved emergency services for people injured in traffic, mountain, and farm accidents, shortening time and distance to the hospital, especially as area highways grew more crowded.

Inset: Life Flight helicopters operated by Intermountain Healthcare provided life-saving transportation to trauma patients in the 1980s.

down and injured passengers would be brought to McKay-Dee. It was the middle of the night and the helicopter-landing pad had not yet been completed.

Mrs. Chard directed the chopper to land on the Professional Building parking lot while employees were quickly directed to park their cars with the headlights pointed to illuminate a large circle. Patients were successfully unloaded from the chopper, and Mrs. Chard recalls the only mishaps were the sheets covering the ER carts and her cap blown away by the wash from the helicopter blades.

LDS CHURCH GIVES HOSPITALS TO THEIR COMMUNITIES

Although the formation of Health Services Corporation by the LDS Church freed up its ecclesiastical leaders for other duties, the ownership and operation of hospitals continued to conflict with the Church's overall mission. HSC Commissioner Dr. James O. Mason remarked, "If we really were concerned about the poor and the needy, where would we build hospitals? Not in Utah. The Church would build hospitals in Tonga, South America, and Central America. If hospitals were essential to the mission of the Church, we had them in the wrong place."

Above: This photo, circa 1973, prompts one's curiosity as to what sort of emergency called for a patient or family member to arrive in the ER parking lot on horseback, particularly in winter.

Right: A few years after the new Thomas D. Dee Memorial Hospital was opened adjacent to the David O. McKay Hospital, a connecting corridor annex was constructed, joining the two hospitals into one.

After several lengthy studies, the Church decided to give up the hospitals into a newly formed, not-for-profit corporation to serve the citizens of the Intermountain Region. The decision to retain a not-for-profit organization for the hospitals ensured that they would continue to be operated as a community asset and provide charity care. At the time, HSC and its 15 hospitals carried a market value of between $250 million and $300 million, but the Church made a donation of them to the new corporation, allowing it to begin operations without significant debt.

Other churches, before and since, have divested hospitals, but no other donation has approximated the size and value of this hospital system to the public.

In September 1974, the Church's First Presidency issued a statement that said in part:

After a thorough study and consideration, the Council of the First Presidency and Quorum of the Twelve Apostles has decided to divert the full efforts of the Health Services of the Church to the health needs of the worldwide Church membership. As a result of that decision and because the operation of hospitals is not central to the mission of the Church, the Church has decided to divest itself of its extensive hospital holdings…The growing worldwide responsibility of the Church makes it difficult to justify provision of curative services in a single, affluent, geographical locality.

Health Care Board

The first step following the divestiture of the hospitals was to create a not-for-profit, community-based hospital system named Intermountain Health Care and to choose a board reflecting the geographic scope of the hospitals and the social and religious diversity of the people they served. Thomas D. Dee II from McKay-Dee was named to the system board as

treasurer and chairman of the finance committee. The new executive committee included William N. Jones as chairman; Dr. Louis Shricker as vice chairman; Robert Bischoff as secretary; and Thomas Dee as treasurer. Dee remembers:

"We looked at each other for a moment and said, 'Now what?' Fortunately, we had some basic education in management and were able to keep some good people who had worked with the system.

"I think it was a bit of a surprise. Everybody expected there might be a greater connection with the Church during the transition. But there was none at all. It was kind of like casting their child adrift in the Nile. But we survived somehow."

Three goals were identified by the Intermountain Health Care Board:

1. To be a global leader and model in healthcare.
2. To be a model alliance of hospital care, physician care, and medical services.
3. To provide the best quality care at the least cost, meeting community needs.

1975: an Outstanding Year of Innovation and Service

In 1975, more patients were admitted, babies born, outpatients served, emergencies met, and surgeries and laboratory work performed than during any previous year.

Emergency room remodeling began. Costs were defrayed by the children of Florence Dee Barker (daughter of Thomas D. and Annie Taylor Dee) and her husband, Judge George Barker. When the remodeling of the ER was completed in 1976, at a cost of $140,000, it was dedicated to Florence.

The hospital opened a gastroenterology laboratory, purchased an ultrasound system, installed a gamma camera in nuclear medicine, added a telemetry monitory system to the coronary care unit, and purchased four more fetal heart-rate monitoring units and eight more vital-sign monitors

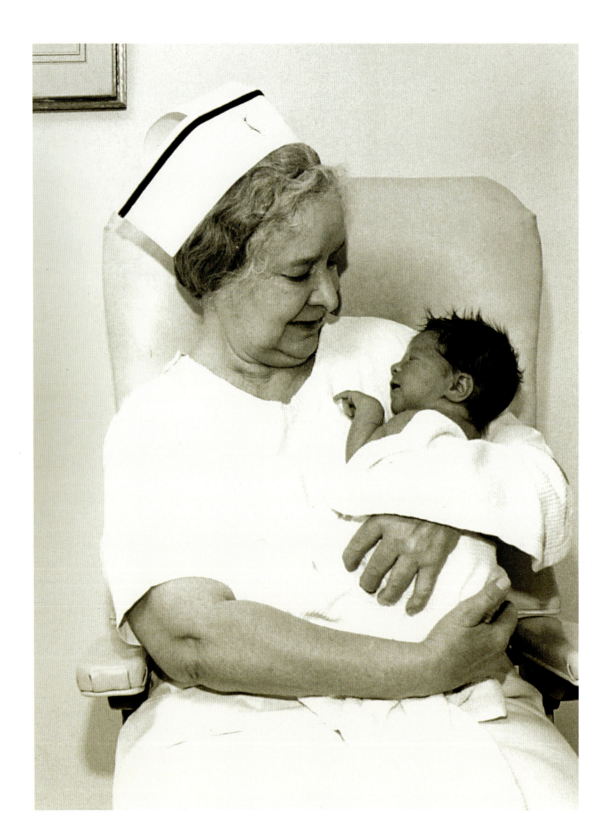

After 40 years of service at the Dee and McKay-Dee hospitals, Louise Scoville, RN, retired in 1974. She graduated from the Thomas D. Dee Memorial Hospital School of Nursing in 1932 and was named Nurse of the Year by the Utah State Nursing Association in 1972. During the final five and a half years of her career, she cared for premature babies.

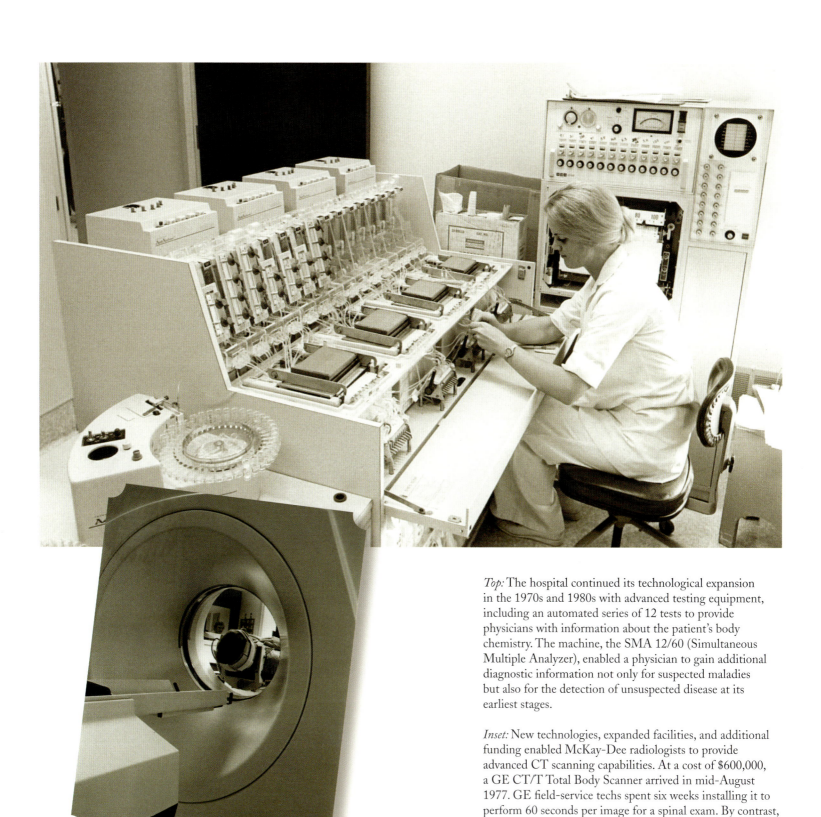

Top: The hospital continued its technological expansion in the 1970s and 1980s with advanced testing equipment, including an automated series of 12 tests to provide physicians with information about the patient's body chemistry. The machine, the SMA 12/60 (Simultaneous Multiple Analyzer), enabled a physician to gain additional diagnostic information not only for suspected maladies but also for the detection of unsuspected disease at its earliest stages.

Inset: New technologies, expanded facilities, and additional funding enabled McKay-Dee radiologists to provide advanced CT scanning capabilities. At a cost of $600,000, a GE CT/T Total Body Scanner arrived in mid-August 1977. GE field-service techs spent six weeks installing it to perform 60 seconds per image for a spinal exam. By contrast, in 2010, 64 images are produced in one-third of a second.

for the Intensive Care Unit and the post-operative recovery room. These innovations supported remarkable healthcare improvements in emergency, critical care, and the delivery of trauma services.

LIFE AND DEATH

In 1976, Rehabilitation Medicine and psychiatric services recorded growth. A fifth physician helped ease the load in the Emergency Room. Births hit an all-time high of 4,210, and three obstetrical anesthesiologists were added to the staff.

The next year, a connecting corridor between the two hospitals' second floors gave McKay better access to the maternity overflow unit in the Dee. This connecting corridor further cemented references joining the hospitals' names into one, McKay-Dee.

On October 4, 1977, the hospital's last remaining founder died. Lawrence T. Dee, 86, had served as a trustee of Thomas D. Dee Memorial Hospital and as a member of the McKay-Dee Governing Board for 55 years. That board adopted a resolution stating Dee "was a man of compassion, a philanthropist who gave of his own means that others might be made well, a gentle critic who urged us on to ever higher goals," as well as "our dearly beloved friend whose passing marks the end of an era."

In December, the hospital received approval to build a structure for rehabilitation medicine, create space for storage and erect a parking terrace, as well as to remodel the former rehab space into an outpatient center. It also received approval for a nursing unit on McKay's sixth floor. Also in 1977, the hospital began using a total body scanner, giving physicians a new and sophisticated diagnostic tool that was capable of taking an image every 60 seconds.

In January 1978, neonatologist W. Richards Weeks, MD, began directing care in the neonatal unit, helping care for sick newborns. Also that year, the hospital acquired the McKay

Professional Building and renamed it in honor of Lawrence T. Dee, the hospital founder who had died the previous year.

The hospital's first outreach facility, the McKay-Dee Medical Clinic, opened at 2400 N. Washington Boulevard on September 25, 1979. The focus of the clinic was to provide physician services after regular office hours — nights, weekends, and holidays.

Meanwhile, the conversion of wards into private patient rooms continued, and the Thomas G. Barker Vascular Laboratory opened to help detect the possibility of strokes in patients. The hospital also acquired a Cell Saver machine, which permits patients to be transfused with their own blood. The process lowers patient costs and reduces the amount of blood needed from the hospital blood bank, keeping enough blood in supply for heart surgery and trauma patients, traditionally the largest blood users in the hospital. It also reduces the risk of infection and saves time because the laboratory work to cross match blood isn't needed.

GREAT STRIDES IN THE 1980S

The hospital continued to grow and change through the 1980s, with H. Gary Pehrson, who had been on McKay-Dee's administrative staff from 1972 to 1977, at the helm. He was tapped to take Kenneth C. Johnson's place after Johnson was named regional administrator for six Intermountain Healthcare hospitals in Idaho and Wyoming in 1980.

Also in 1980, a remodeling of Pediatrics opened up space for an intermediate care unit, and the Stewart Rehabilitation Center was dedicated in honor of longtime hospital supporters Donnel B. and Elizabeth S. Stewart. The rehab facility featured a therapy pool ranging from 2.5 feet to 4.5 feet deep and was heated to 100 degrees for the approximately 30 percent of rehabilitation patients needing therapeutic exercises. Parallel bars could be added to support patients relearning how to walk. A treatment table could be

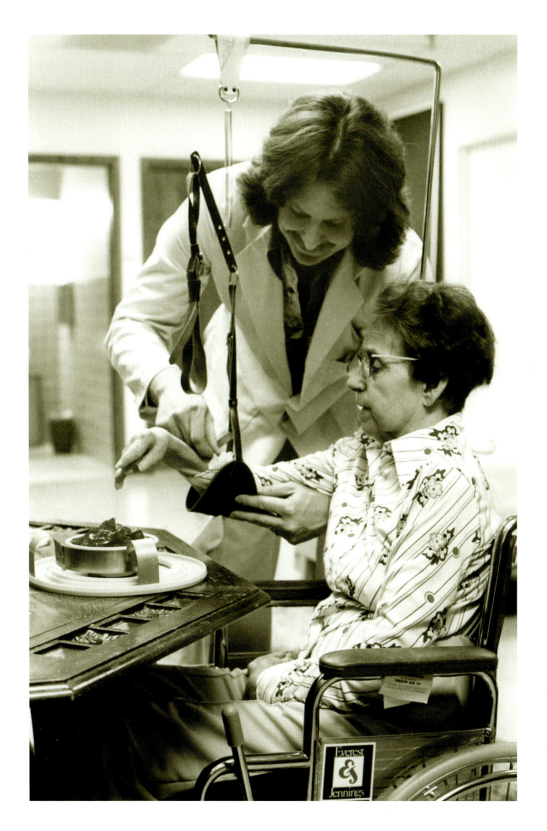

McKay-Dee's rehabilitation services made great strides during the '70s and '80s. Ronald L. Herrick, administrative director of the McKay-Dee Rehabilitation Center, explained in 1979 that "a team approach is used to treat all rehab patients. We treat the whole patient, not just parts of the patient." Pictured, Ben DeHaan, Occupational Therapist, assists a patient.

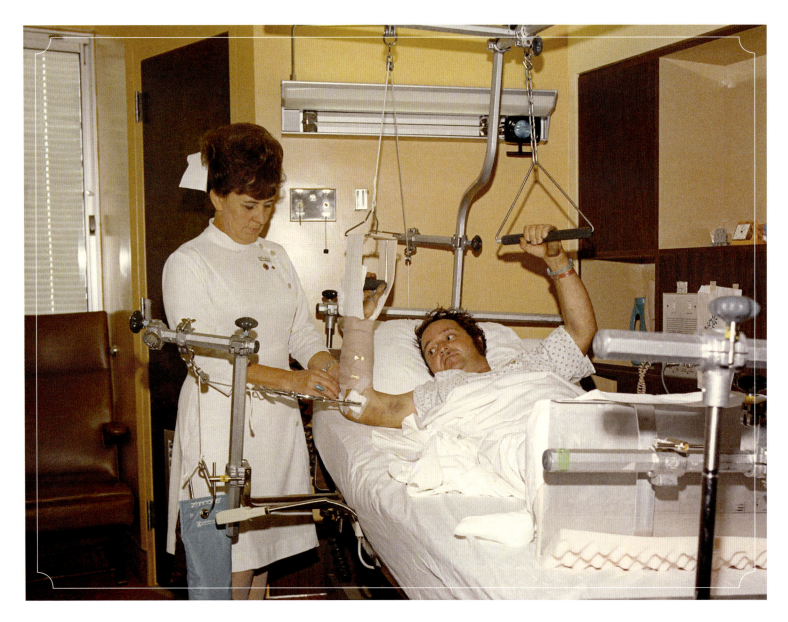

During the '80s and '90s, McKay-Dee Hospital was known for its excellent care and treatment of severely injured patients. The Donnel B. and Elizabeth S. Stewart Rehabilitation Center greatly advanced the ability of caregivers to provide rehabilitation therapy using the latest innovations.

lowered into the water for range-of-motion exercises, and whirlpools were at one end of the pool.

"The benefits of water are numerous," Ron Herrick, Rehabilitation Administrative Director, said in a 1980 employee newsletter. "Its buoyancy helps sustain someone who cannot walk when he is not in the pool. The hydrostatic pressure of resistance helps strengthen muscles. The heat improves circulation, relieves pain, and is relaxing."

The new facility also included a gym for cardiac rehab patients. The center brought together, for the first time, physicians, psychologists, therapists, social workers, speech pathologists, and vocational counselors to offer personalized care for each patient.

The Occupational Therapy department of the center featured a day living training area where patients could relearn skills needed in the home. A kitchen, bathroom, bedroom, and dining area allowed the patient to practice personal hygiene, dressing, eating, and cooking. Local businesses donated furniture, appliances, carpeting, and other supplies to give the area a more homelike feel.

In 1981, McKay-Dee began a psychiatric crisis intervention program, with a team on duty 24 hours a day, seven days a week, to help patients who came into the Emergency Room for help or were referred by families, friends or physicians. Another program was set up for those not requiring hospitalization or unable to afford psychiatric care. The outpatient program provided regular counseling appointments at the hospital. The crisis intervention team provided psychiatrists with invaluable information from a checklist and could determine if the patient's behavior was episodic by tracking previous visits to the Emergency Room.

Also in 1981, an Outpatient Surgical Center with one-stop outpatient services was built at a cost of $250,000. One area handled admitting, testing, surgery, recovery, and discharge, making procedures easier and more convenient for patients. That year, 35 percent of surgeries performed at McKay-Dee were done on an outpatient basis, compared with just seven percent a few years earlier.

In 1982, McKay-Dee purchased $53,350 in laser equipment. Neurosurgeons, gynecologists and doctors specializing in ears, nose and throat used the equipment, which destroyed rather than removed tissue. The March/April 1984 McKay-Dee employee newsletter listed such benefits as reduced bleeding, smaller incision, and increased accuracy. Lasers erased tattoos, bleached port-wine birthmarks, treated skin cancers and endometriosis, and removed tumors, all without destroying healthy tissue.

In 1983, McKay-Dee began using a new treatment that had just been approved by the Food and Drug Administration. An enzyme extracted from the papaya plant and injected into a herniated disk shrank the disk and relieved pain because it relieved pressure on the nerve. The procedure was successful about 80 percent of the time, involved less risk and cost than surgery, and required a shorter hospital stay.

Also in 1983, the hospital was in the throes of expansion and remodeling. A $6 million project enlarged and updated the Neonatal Intensive Care Unit, the Intensive Care Unit, and the coronary care and stroke units. An intermediate care unit was built for patients who were not critically ill but required more monitoring and attention than patients in regular hospital rooms. This allowed patients to pay less than they would for ICU care and gave the ICU more room for patients in critical condition. One of the country's top authorities in critical care design was hired to facilitate the changes at McKay-Dee.

Under McKay-Dee Administrator H. Gary Pehrson, the hospital began to focus on care for seriously ill patients. Contributing to the change was increased automobile accidents, poor eating patterns, increased stress and the fact that previously traditional hospital care could be done more cheaply outside of the hospital, such as in outpatient surgery. With more outpatient surgeries and shorter hospital stays, the hospital began to focus on critical care that patients could not find elsewhere. McKay-Dee served as a referral center for critically ill patients in Northern Utah, Southern Idaho and Western Wyoming. That year, according to an employee newsletter, 15 percent of ICU patients, 13 percent of coronary care unit patients, and 25 percent of NICU patients were referred to McKay-Dee from outlying areas.

In July 1984, McKay-Dee's NICU staff started a follow-up clinic to monitor NICU babies through age six, providing free six-month checkups and visits with a developmental specialist, speech pathologist, social worker, pediatric nutritionist, audiologist, ophthalmologist, and pulmonary therapist. Parents received advice to aid in their child's development, and children with serious problems were referred to a specialist. The fact that the service was free is significant, as babies from lower socioeconomic groups accounted for 25 percent to 40 percent of NICU admissions, Rod Fifield, a clinical social worker, said in an employee newsletter. Premature births in lower socioeconomic groups were more likely because their mothers often couldn't afford prenatal care, he said.

In 1985, McKay-Dee began an equestrian program for those with disabilities. Co-sponsored by Easter Seals, it offered recreation but also produced therapeutic effects. Volunteers donated their time and their horses one afternoon a week, May through August. McKay-Dee Stewart Rehabilitation Center physical therapist Stephen Spencer, the man behind the equestrian program, reported reduced spasms in those with cerebral palsy, better balance and coordination, increased endurance and strength, improved mobility and posture, and improved cardiovascular function because of increased adrenaline flow.

"But the best benefit is that it's great fun," he said in a 1986 employee newsletter. "These people have a chance to get out of their wheelchairs. They have freedom from their immobility. They really thought it was great; some craved it."

In 1986, Gary Pehrson made regional vice president, and Thomas F. Hanrahan took his place as CEO of McKay-Dee. The new McKay-Dee outpatient surgical center and professional office building opened. On June 5, 1986, McKay-Dee also opened the only pediatric rehabilitation program north of Primary Children's Medical Center in Salt Lake City. It integrated all disciplines of therapy, constantly changing and improving treatment to best fit each child's needs. Operated jointly by the Stewart Rehabilitation Center and Primary Children's Rehabilitation Center, the new facility served children challenged with congenital defects, developmental delays, accidental injuries, or debilitating illness. The McKay-Dee Pediatric Rehabilitation Center also worked closely with the school system and helped prepare special-needs children for the challenges they could face in school. Staff helped youths build self-esteem and set goals before starting school and, once the child was attending classes, worked with teachers and school counselors to address any problems or concerns.

"It's tougher to work with kids, but also more rewarding," Monica McCaskey, Director of the McKay-Dee Pediatric Rehabilitation Center, said in the summer 1991 employee newsletter. "There's the emotional part of it. Sometimes you think, 'It's just not right, it's not fair that someone so young would have to deal with such serious problems.' But it gives you a feeling of accomplishment to know that you are improving their chances in life, even though it's sometimes hard."

June 1987 saw the opening of the McKay-Dee Institute for Behavioral Health, which treated children and adults on an inpatient or outpatient basis for a number of disorders, including depression, eating disorders, and anxiety.

In January 1989, McKay-Dee began the Optifast weight-loss program and reported excellent results in the first year.

Facing: Jennifer Edmonds, daughter of Mr. and Mrs. Jerold K. Edmonds, was a rehabilitation patient from 1975 until this photo in the '80s, showing her able to walk with her quad canes.

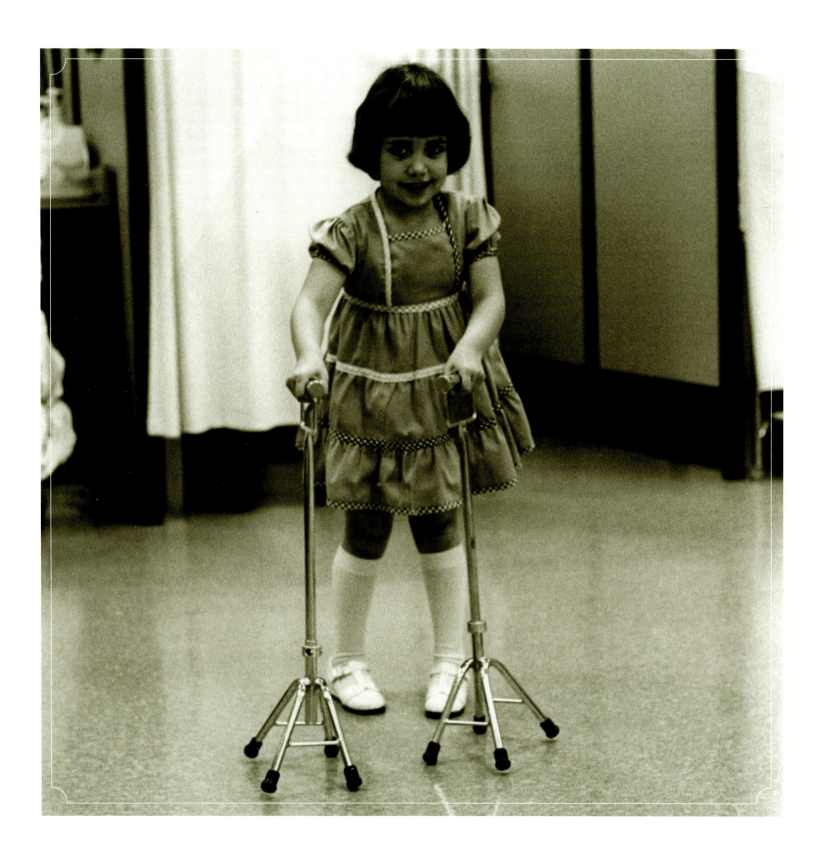

The highly researched program for the severely obese featured a liquid, high-protein diet. Medical supervision ensured patient safety as participants underwent 12 weeks of fasting — consuming only the liquid protein diet. As participants fasted, they attended behavior-modification classes so they would be successful when food and exercise were added to the regimen. Research showed 80 percent of patients who continued the program for a year did not regain more than a third of their weight in 72 months. The program also benefited diabetics and those with high blood pressure.

A 1989 employee newsletter featured the newly opened McKay-Dee Heart Institute, which put heart patient services in one central location. Heart catheterizations had jumped from 582 in 1983 to 1,217 in 1988. Patient numbers were increasing as medical advances expanded treatment options. The institute fostered cooperation among doctors, surgery staff, post-op, nurses, emergency workers, respiratory care, cardiac rehabilitation, and technicians. The institute featured two catheterization labs, two operating-room suites, testing rooms, and support staff. It also collected data for studies that will help evaluate treatment and provide information for research. The hospital's role was expanded to Northern Utah, Southern Idaho and Western Wyoming. McKay-Dee became a referral center, with its cardiologists consulting with physicians at smaller rural hospitals.

GIVING AND GROWING IN THE 1990S

In 1990, seven employees, six nurses and seven physicians from McKay-Dee were called up to serve in Operation Desert Storm. The hospital established a support group for hospital employees with deployed friends and family members.

In 1991, McKay-Dee Administrator Tom Hanrahan presented a $5,000 check from the Intermountain Healthcare Foundation to underwrite Your Community Connection's Rape Crisis Center programs in Ogden. The money helped provide counseling to rape victims and helped pay for rape kits used for collecting evidence for prosecuting perpetrators, but also went toward education and prevention programs in the community. McKay-Dee had presented YCC with a $2,000 check the year before, and in 1991, the YCC honored McKay-Dee as an Employer of the Year.

Also that year, a McKay-Dee clinical engineering employee, Jim Anderson, went to Armenia to help set up equipment for a country devastated and still recovering from an earthquake in 1988. Intermountain Healthcare had donated more than 9,200 pounds of medical supplies, and Anderson helped set up ventilators, defibrillators, ultrasonic imagers, and other equipment, then — with the help of interpreters — taught Soviet technicians how to use the equipment.

McKay-Dee also presented a $13,000 check to underwrite the DARE program in Ogden schools. That check covered all expenses for a year of the program, teaching children self-esteem and how to say no to drugs and alcohol. "As a hospital, we constantly face the devastating effects of drug and alcohol use in the Emergency Room and in our treatment programs," Hanrahan said in a 1991 employee newsletter. "We have a responsibility to educate our next generation of youths about the dangers of drugs and alcohol."

That year, the hospital celebrated the installation of an MRI, and remodeling of the Stewart Rehabilitation Center and L.T. Dee pharmacy continued. Staff offices were relocated to create space for treating head injuries.

In 1992, Terri Kane, McKay-Dee's Nurse Manager of Women's and Children's Services, received the Nursing Excellence Award. In the hospital Neonatal Intensive Care Unit, she had developed an orientation program that became the corporate model and helped develop the Sibling Support Group, which was patented and nationally recognized. She secured funds and developed the Neonatal Outcome Clinic and brought the Gastroesophageal Reflux Program and the Percutaneous Line Placement Program to McKay-Dee.

Also in 1992, "Rescue 911" taped scenes at McKay-Dee and aired the show nationally on CBS. Even though the Emergency Department was under construction, staff and physicians re-enacted scenes — or worked behind the scenes — to demonstrate the care that was given to an Idaho State Police trooper.

A six-level parking deck for 617 vehicles opened in 1993. It featured a handicapped-accessible elevator, an enclosed walkway to the hospital, and a video security system, as well as regular security patrols. The Surgical Center added an operating room and eight recovery bays. The hospital's Heart Team was nationally recognized, first in CBS medical reporter Bob Arnot's book, "*The Best Medicine: How to Choose the Top Doctors, the Top Hospitals and the Top Treatments,*" and second, in *Fortune* magazine. Also, in April of that year, McKay-Dee's quality efforts as an Intermountain Healthcare facility were featured on the Discovery Channel.

In 1995, the American College of Radiology granted McKay-Dee's mammography program accreditation. The hospital had two mammography machines, one of which was the only machine in Northern Utah designed to scan dense breast tissue. At that time, a 1995 employee newsletter reported, one in nine women would develop breast cancer in her lifetime, and early detection was essential. To receive accreditation, staff qualifications, equipment, quality control, and quality-assurance programs had to meet rigid standards, as did image quality and amount of radiation. McKay-Dee was meeting its goal of providing the best possible mammographic exam with the lowest possible risk to the patient.

That year, McKay-Dee joined other Intermountain Healthcare facilities in implementing a sophisticated laboratory computer system that streamlined test results, improved information formatting, and provided information to caregivers more quickly. Results could be transmitted electronically to physician offices and, in the future, transmit results to the electronic patient record, which acts as a lifetime clinical repository for Intermountain Healthcare patients. The change brought more quality and efficiency to Intermountain Healthcare labs.

Also in 1995, the McKay-Dee Women and Children's Services department began a program called Mother's Choice, which allowed new mothers to decide whether to keep their baby with them in their newly remodeled postpartum room or have their child cared for in the nursery, also newly remodeled. The same caregiver would be responsible for both mother and child, facilitating teaching and learning, as well as increasing customer satisfaction.

That year, McKay-Dee Registered Nurse Karen Miller joined eight other Intermountain Healthcare employees in a trip to Shantou, in mainland China, with Operation Smile. The 44 volunteers paid their own way to serve a medical mission to benefit children with facial anomalies. KSL Channel 5 produced a 30-minute documentary about the team's efforts.

The hospital was recognized at the 12th Annual Healthcare Advertising Awards, also in 1995. McKay-Dee won a silver in the newspaper ad category and a bronze in the outdoor/billboard category for its "Nationally Ranked" campaign.

Internationally, 1995 was also a big year. Hospital CEO Thomas Hanrahan joined the Utah 2002 Olympic Games delegation in Budapest, Hungary. Intermountain Healthcare had donated a substantial amount toward the effort to host the 2002 Winter Games, and Intermountain Healthcare and McKay-Dee were thrilled when it was announced that Utah would host the games. McKay-Dee would later be named to provide hospital care during the 2002 Winter Olympics, and Intermountain Healthcare would be named by the Salt Lake Organizing Committee as the healthcare provider for the games.

In January 2000, McKay-Dee Hospital Center was recognized as one of the best hospitals in an eight-state mountain region by HICA. The Healthcare Informatics Consulting & Compliance Agency, according to its web site, is a community-based, informational delivery system for healthcare organizations and individuals who desire to learn about health-related, informed decision-making. The agency annually conducts surveys of hospitals across the country to determine its top picks.

An Aging Ogden Icon

It was a landmark at the heart of the community. For 33 years, McKay-Dee stood gleaming white, offering hope and healing to thousands of patients and their families.

The hospital had been built in an era of extended patient stays in the '70s and '80s, but by the late '90s, nearly 50 percent of patrons visited the hospital for outpatient services. The board and administrators were faced with making significant, difficult, and costly changes to the building.

Finally, however, it was the realization that the hospital was structurally deficient and unable to withstand even a moderate earthquake that accelerated plans for a new McKay-Dee. Most notably, both the 1987 Loma Prieta earthquake, also known as the World Series earthquake, which struck the San Francisco Bay Area on October 17, 1989, and the 1994 Northridge (California) earthquake registering 6.9 magnitude in Los Angeles called acute attention to the situation. In an effort to assure the highest-quality healthcare and the safety of patients, staff, and visitors, Intermountain Healthcare's local region administrators hired local seismic engineers to assess the building's viability to withstand a Wasatch Fault earthquake.

The Utah assessment determined that McKay-Dee was not seismically sound and damage would be devastating. The board and administrators were at first skeptical, but with the Ogden area on a known fault, seismic experts from California were engaged to make a further assessment. Their results were even more alarming than the local determinations. The San Francisco seismic professionals reported that the structural condition of McKay-Dee was nothing short of a catastrophic disaster waiting to happen. Both boards of McKay-Dee Hospital Center and Intermountain Healthcare agreed that these sobering warnings could not be ignored.

Added to the growing need for more space for monitoring equipment in patient rooms and the evolution of technology in every service line of medical care, these seismic assessments of the McKay-Dee facility underscored the urgency for a new hospital complex built as a safer and more technologically flexible structure.

A New Hospital for the Ages

On August 28, 1997, Intermountain Healthcare and McKay-Dee officials announced plans to build a new hospital – this one on 63 acres about two blocks south of the first McKay-Dee Hospital Center campus. Neighbors surrounding the area proposed for the new hospital showed their support, and the Ogden City Planning Commission and Ogden City Council approved the necessary rezone that would allow the project to move forward.

A Dallas-based architectural company, H.K.S., was selected to develop the hospital plans. In 1996, the firm – which has ties to the local design group Design West – had been ranked No. 1 in the United States for total dollars spent on new health-care facilities. With at least 950 employees, it is the largest architectural firm in the country. It has designed a number of stadiums and corporate offices around the United States, as well as the U.S. Census Bureau Headquarters in Maryland, the Children's Medical Center and the Texas Scottish Rite Hospital, both in Dallas, and the Winchester Medical Center in Virginia.

Playing a large role in McKay-Dee's design was the possibility of a devastating earthquake along the Wasatch Front in the next 50 years. The hospital would be built by Ogden-based Big-D Construction to remain operational during and after a seismic event. A welded steel frame and beam-tocolumn connections would allow the new facility at 4401 Harrison Boulevard to be flexible as tremors shudder through the ground and into the structure. Engineers from the University of Utah conducted seismic testing to guide the structural design of the facility to meet all current and Uniform Building Code requirements. In fact, even though the International Building Codes were set to change in 2003, a year after the hospital opened, McKay-Dee administrators decided to meet even the proposed codes so the facility would comply with future needs and expectations.

While work on the new McKay-Dee continued, ground was officially broken on November 8, 2000, for the Child Development Center northwest of the main facility on the new hospital campus, thanks to a generous gift by the Swanson Family Foundation. The Foundation covered the entire $1.2 million in construction costs for the 9,000-square-foot center, as well as a playground. The current facility accommodated 65 students, but the new building would accommodate 122.

All fundraisers, hospital administrators and employees, volunteers, area residents, and patients were anxious to have a new hospital that promised to be as much of an icon as the first McKay-Dee Hospital Center, as well as the Thomas D. Dee Memorial Hospital before it. The new campus would also set a new benchmark for medical facilities across the country. ❧

Dr. Paul Southwick, who specialized in internal medicine, is seen descending the dramatic stairwell of the east-facing McKay Hospital entrance in the '70s. "I didn't use the elevators during my years at the McKay," says Dr. Southwick. "When I first stood at the top of those stairs and looked out at the beautiful Wasatch peaks, I felt overcome to be serving in such a wonderful new facility. I was brought to tears at the thought of what all we medical people would be able to do for our patients in more efficient spaces and with the latest technology. I wanted to be around to enjoy that view and to be of help for many years, so doing rounds I made it my practice to hurry up and down those stairs to keep my heart strong."

McKAY-DEE HOSPI

THOMAS D. DEE
MEMORIAL HOSPITAL

A New Hospital
for a New Millennium
→ 2002 *to* 2010 ←

Part of the strength of Annie Taylor Dee's legacy is its focus on providing the means and tools clinicians need to provide the highest-quality healthcare. In 1997, it became evident that the existing facility was falling behind. Structural shortcomings left it vulnerable to natural disasters. The layout of the facility didn't accommodate the changing nature of patient healthcare. An increasing number of services were being provided on an outpatient basis, and patients admitted to the hospital were coming largely for acute care. The care providers were also embracing a new concept of service focused on healing the whole patient; this concept expanded to include prevention programs. As a result, intense planning to provide a new hospital began calling upon extensive resources, both nationally and locally, culminating in the new Intermountain McKay-Dee Hospital Center, which opened at 4401 Harrison Boulevard in 2002. Just as Annie Taylor Dee and her advisors began studying hospitals around the county in preparation for the design of the Dee Hospital a hundred years ago, a new team of managers, inspired by Annie's example, set out to develop a different kind of community hospital for the 21st century.

The hospital's founding families celebrated the opening of the McKay-Dee Hospital Center on March 20, 2002. Thomas D. Dee II, Thomas D. Dee III, and Edward McKay, MD, represented two Ogden-area families dedicated to improving the health and well-being of their community.

View of Intermountain McKay-Dee Hospital
Center at 4401 Harrison Boulevard from
southwest of the campus. To the east are the
Wasatch Mountains, to the west, the valley and
Great Salt Lake.

After years of planning and preparation, the new Intermountain McKay-Dee Hospital Center was ready to open. Patients, caregivers, visitors, and vendors found the hospital attractive and inviting, a visible manifestation of how far hospital facilities had come in a hundred years.

CUTTING THE RIBBON, OPENING THE DOORS

The opening of the Intermountain McKay-Dee Hospital campus was heralded with cheers, fireworks and the cutting of a red ribbon on March 20, 2002.

McKay-Dee CEO Thomas Hanrahan; Intermountain Healthcare President Bill Nelson; McKay-Dee Board Chairman Paul Kunz; Thomas D. Dee II and Thomas D. Dee III, McKay-Dee board members and descendants of hospital founder Annie Taylor Dee; Edward McKay, MD, son of the late LDS Church President David O. McKay; and Intermountain Healthcare Board Chairman and Ogden native Richard J. Galbraith helped cut the ribbon.

Speaking to the crowd, Hanrahan praised the work of employee committees, architects, contractors, and Intermountain Healthcare officials who helped the new hospital campus become a reality.

"If you want to know what Intermountain Healthcare does with its earnings, you are about to see it," he said.

Hanrahan went on to thank employees and other donors who contributed to the McKay-Dee Hospital Foundation's capital campaign, raising $15 million of the $190 million cost of building the new facility.

"Hospitals can be unpleasant places. People come in and give up their clothes, dignity, and sense of control, but we set out to change all that. This place was built for comfort, harmony, and healing."

Thomas Dee III told the audience that his grandfather, in whose memory the first Dee hospital was built, would be "proud as a new papa." With the Dee and McKay family names, this new facility is the only hospital in the Intermountain Healthcare system with a family name. "We are grateful Intermountain Healthcare kept the family names for this hospital," Thomas Dee III said.

Edward McKay told those gathered he believed his father,

Participating in the ribbon-cutting are *back, from left:* Tom Hanrahan, McKay-Dee Hospital CEO; Thomas D. (Tim) Dee III; *front, from left:* Bill Nelson, Intermountain Healthcare President; Paul T. Kunz, Chairman, McKay-Dee Board of Trustees; Thomas D. Dee II, Richard J. Galbraith, Intermountain Healthcare Board Chairman; Edward McKay, MD, and Utah Lt. Gov. Olene Walker.

who helped the Dee hospital survive in 1915 under the banner of the Church, would be impressed as well. "He would have been thrilled to see this building with all this latest technology, and he always responded to beauty. I know he would be pleased and humbled with this marvel."

And though the hospital facility is a wonder to behold and has a long and impressive history, Kunz captured what would make the hospital truly remarkable to patients putting their lives in McKay-Dee's hands: its people.

"Will this be a great healing center? We have the technology to do it, but it takes more than that. All truly great medical centers have a spiritual quality to their treatment. It requires caregivers to share their inner qualities," he said. "I hope each caregiver and employee of this facility will come with kindness, compassion, and quality of character. This institution will receive its greatness from the character of its people."

After years of planning and construction, moving day came. Months of planning had gone into this day under the leadership of Julie Huntley, RN, Chief of Nursing at the time. There were many decisions to be made and challenges to face in moving not just patients but all the equipment needed to take care of them. To our delight, it all went off like clockwork. Many community agencies, including fire departments and community ambulances, helped with the transfers as we moved one group after another. Finally, we had a nearly empty hospital as we made one last trip through the old building. Two patients were left: a woman in labor we didn't want to move until her baby was safely delivered, and another woman who'd had an emergency appendectomy and was still in recovery. By 2 p.m., everyone was transferred safely and all tucked into our wonderful new facility.

—Richard Arbogast, MD, Chief Medical Officer

On March 25, 2002, 150 McKay-Dee Hospital patients were moved to the new facility with the assistance of a national moving company. The move began just before 6 a.m. Eight ambulances lined up at the Emergency Department to conduct the 10-minute transport, which began with the most critical patients. Many staff and administrators remembered the move in 1969 from the Dee to the McKay Hospital and the logistical challenges of safeguarding their patients. Elective procedures had been canceled the week before, but at least one baby proved uncooperative and became the last baby born at the old hospital. That last baby, a girl, arrived at 5:44 a.m., and the new McKay-Dee welcomed its first baby, also a girl, at 11:29 a.m.

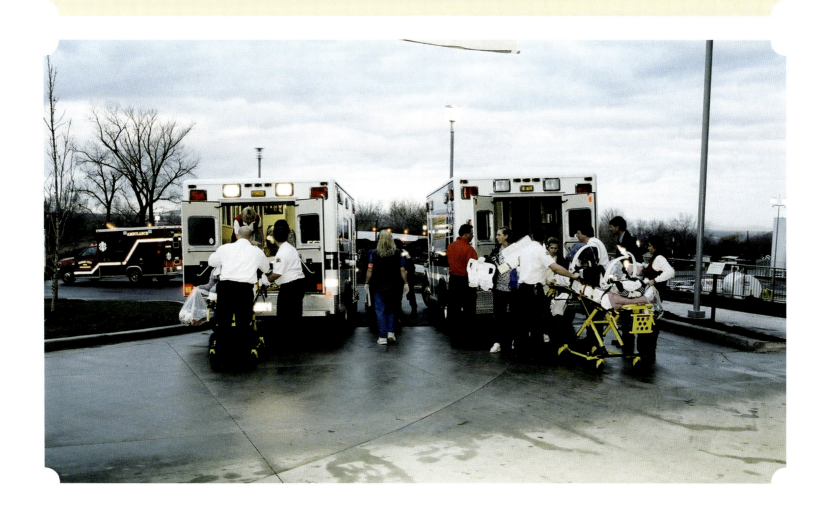

CREATING A HEALING ENVIRONMENT

The dream became a reality. "The new hospital didn't look or feel like any hospital where I had ever worked," recalls Bonnie L. Jacklin, RN, MSN, and chief nursing officer. Jacklin, who along with many others had been involved in the design and planning of the new McKay-Dee, said each person involved now had an opportunity to make a mark on the new facility.

"Our purpose was to build a healing environment that would augment and support the technical science of healthcare," she said.

Jacklin, who was the Destination Move Director on moving day, welcomed and assigned all patients transferring from the former McKay-Dee to the new hospital. She said, "I will always remember the day this hospital was brought to life."

Among the first activities the hospital's planners initiated was a Healing Environment Task Force to tap into the knowledge of national experts, local nurses, physicians, hospital administrators, and the public. From these interviews, nine priorities were identified:

1. PRIVACY AND EMOTIONAL COMFORT

Patients, their guests and hospital staff can find solitude in the Harold and Shirley Mack Family Chapel and the E. Rich and Jane Brewer Meditation Room on the second floor of the atrium near the Harold J. Mack Intensive Care Unit and the Dr. Louis Scowcroft Peery Foundation Surgery Unit. The chapel features a peaceful pastoral scene in stained glass, as well as inspirational literature. A half-hour LDS Church service is offered at the hospital on Sunday mornings.

2. Family Accommodations

Patient rooms are large enough for patients, their families, and friends to visit while providing caregivers enough space to attend to the patients' needs.

3. Lighting and Windows

The shape and position of the building was designed to enhance the views of the surrounding valley and nearby mountains. Windows are larger than normal to increase the flow of natural light into patient rooms, and skylights line the main public corridor.

4. Wayfinding

In addition to a single, large public corridor designed for patients to move through the hospital, services were thoughtfully co-located to minimize patient movement and reduce confusion. In addition, McKay-Dee Hospital utilizes a parallel-corridor system. The outer corridor is an open and airy public thoroughfare with many windows looking out on gardens. Located on that open corridor are waiting areas and information desks for each department and the entrances to all professional offices. The inner corridor system is a private staff and patient area. This essential passageway is kept clear for physicians, nurses, and other caregivers to quickly move equipment and supplies to their patients. The parallel-corridor system assures that transferring vulnerable patients from surgical and recovery areas to their rooms is safe and private.

5. Communications and Access to Information

The hospital's Community Health and Information Center, sponsored by the Samuel C. and Myra Powell Foundation, is on the first floor adjacent to the Patient Tower's entrance, providing easy access to information regarding diagnosis and treatment. The center has information about wellness and safety classes, seminars and more. Information is also available in Spanish.

6. Sound

A "nurse call" paging system facilitates communication on an "on-demand" basis among physicians and other clinicians, or patients and their caregivers. The public is largely shielded from intercom communication, which reduces stress and allows patients to rest with less interruption.

In the Main Lobby, a grand piano is played throughout the day by local volunteers, organized by the McKay-Dee Hospital Foundation. The music played by volunteers known as the Piano Guild creates a welcoming environment to calm the nerves of people seeking care.

7. AIR QUALITY

Patients and visitors are ensured clean, temperature-adjusted air, and a pleasant natural scent, enhanced by the building's open design. Live plants also act as natural air filters.

8. VIEWS OF NATURE/ARTWORK

Patient rooms overlook the healing gardens. Windows reveal sweeping views of the mountains to the east, the valley to the west. Large landscape paintings line the hallways, elegant bouquets of flowers decorate countertops, and planters of lush greenery dot the main corridor and waiting areas.

9. COLOR

The natural beauty of Utah is represented with a warm color scheme. Instead of sterile white walls, patrons are greeted by wood and warm earth tones in wall coverings, paint colors, fixtures, and furniture. The plants and flowers add splashes of color.

Enter the McKay-Dee Hospital Center's Main Lobby today, and it is clear that it is a different experience. From the ground up, the new hospital was designed with the patient in mind. Hospital CEO Tim Pehrson says, "First impressions do matter. The public will find neither dark winding corridors here, nor wards with many patients all in one room. There's one big 'spine' to the building with a north and south corridor to help patients, staff, and visitors flow through the building with little confusion."

Left and above: In the main lobby of the hospital, local volunteers, organized by the McKay-Dee Hospital Foundation, play a grand piano throughout the day. Patients and their guests can relax in comfortable chairs and sofas set around a large fireplace.

Chapel Room — A Quiet Place for Comfort

Intermountain McKay-Dee Hospital Center's mission to be a place of healing for life would not be a full-rounded facility without an indoor place to meditate, pray, grieve, or rest at any hour of the day or night. The simple and comforting chapel room has a stabling influence on patients, family, and caregivers, including hospital personnel who deal with daily emotional stress as part of their job.

The hospital has a volunteer pastoral-care program with counseling clergy available for scheduled or on-call service for patient and family support. These caregivers know meeting spiritual needs is an important part of treating patients either making their way through the healing process, undergoing the stresses of illness, or facing – and possibly fearing – the dying process. Hundreds of individuals seek necessary solace in this quiet and attractive chapel room.

Now-retired Director of Social Services Rod Fifield says, "Our hospital crisis team is strictly a volunteer team. We follow our hospital's healing commitments. Our goal is to provide spiritual and emotional support to patients and families throughout their stay, as well as end-of-life care, as it needs to be provided."

The McKay-Dee
"Customer Experience"

Intermountain McKay-Dee offers a number of amenities designed to enhance patients' overall experience:

Admission/Registration: Patients can complete their admission and registration processes in one, easily accessible location. Pre-registration can be done online or by phone to facilitate a smooth check-in process.

Outpatients: The Diagnostics Testing area is on the first floor inside the Main Lobby, where patients can receive such basic services as chest X-rays, lab work, preoperative testing, and nutrition counseling.

Interior Design: Design features include a water wall in the visitor entrance, fireplace in the main lobby, planters separating waiting spaces, and comfortable furnishings.

This page: Visitors, particularly parents bringing children to the hospital, appreciate the kind welcome and helpfulness of receptionists who assist them with filling out forms and answering questions. Volunteers Cheryl Scott and Marilyn Enz (retired) make everyone feel welcome. Many elegant bouquets decorate the counters and green plants dot the corridor, reducing the sterile look often seen in hospitals.

Facing: From the Dr. Louis Scowcroft Peery Main lobby, visitors can easily see the focus of each floor of the hospital and enjoy the music volunteers play on the grand piano.

Intermountain McKay-Dee Hospital Center, Floor by Floor

PATIENT TOWER

Size:	*161,848 square feet*
Location:	*South end of the hospital*
Floors:	*Five*

Level 1 — *Behavioral Health; Acute Inpatient Services- children and adults, Food and Nutrition Services, Mountain View Café and Grill, Mary L. Barker Waterfall Lobby, Education Center including Intermountain University and the Edith Dee Green Auditorium, Hospital Library and the Community Health Information Center*

Level 2 — *Mary Elizabeth Dee Shaw Foundation Stewart Inpatient Rehabilitation and Joint and Spine Unit*

Level 3 — *D. Wade Mack Cardiovascular Patient Unit and Intermediate Care*

Level 4 — *Samuel H. and Marian K. Barker Family Women's and Children's Patient Care Unit*

Level 5 — *Medical and Pediatrics, Dr. Ezekiel R. and Edna Wattis Dumke Surgery Patient Care Unit*

Features: — *Complementing the healing environment, waiting and lounge areas and educational facilities were generously gifted in the Patient Tower by donors including: Gordon and June Aldous, J.R. (Joe) and Billie Day, Tim and Candace Dee, Dr. O. Ernest & Jeanette C. Grua , John and Anne Hansen family, Richard K. & Shirley S. Hemingway Foundation, McKay-Dee Hospital employees, Gerald and Cynthia Naylor, Hank and Betty Nowak, Jay C. and Dee Ann Nye, Samuel C. & Myra Powell Foundation, Clark L. Rich MD, Dick and Judy Webber, and the Rotary Club of Ogden.*

DIAGNOSTIC & TREATMENT CENTER

Size:	*233,538 square feet*
Location:	*West side of the hospital*
Floors:	*Four*

Lower Level: — *Pharmacy, Materials Management, Housekeeping, Central Sterile, Family Practice Residency Program, Information Services/Clinical Information Systems, Clinical Engineering*

Level 1	Willard and Ruth Eccles Emergency Department; Mary Elizabeth Dee Shaw Emergency Department West Wing, Glen Mack Family Emergency Extension, Imaging, Laboratory, Val and Ann Browning Cancer Center, Radiation Therapy
Level 2	Harold J. Mack Intensive Care Unit, Dr. Louis Scowcroft Peery Surgical Unit, Surgery Operating Room, Pre-Operation and Post Acute Care Unit
Level 3	George S. and Dolores Dore' Eccles Heart Institute, Alice Barker Hetzel Cardiac Rehabilitation, Administration, Accounting and Finance, Medical Records
Level 4	Labor and Delivery, Newborn Intensive Care Unit

Features: Efficient and comfortable waiting and lounge areas along with consult and procedure rooms were generously gifted by donors including: Gordon and June Aldous, Bank of Utah, Big-D Construction, E. Rich and Jane Brewer, J. Clyde and Eleanor Buehler, J.R. (Joe) and Billie Day, Janice Johnston Dee, Elliot-Hall, Dr. Merrill and Mrs. Evelyn Godfrey, Jim and Jodee Hoellein and Brittnee McMickell, Thomas and Patricia Hanrahan family, Paul T. and Sharee Kunz, Jack and Jodi Livingood, McKay-Dee Hospital employees, McKay-Dee Hospital volunteers, Roy C. and Marilyn C. Nelson, Jay C. and Dee Ann Nye, Theodore G. and Marion MacKay Schmidt, SummitOne Credit Union, James and Marion Whetton, and the W.R. White Company.

PHYSICIAN OFFICES

Size:	179,352 square feet
Location:	East side of the hospital
Floors:	Four

Level 1	Dee Family Main Hospital Lobby, Lawrence Taylor Dee (LTD) Pharmacy, hospital-based services: Human Resources, Public Relations, McKay-Dee Hospital Foundation, Volunteers, Patient Account Services, Quick Diagnostic and Treatment, physician offices, and Medical Oncology
Level 2	Hospital-based services: Neurology Diagnostic Lab, Gastrointestinal Lab, physician offices
Level 3	Physician offices
Level 4	Physician offices, Mammography, Perinatology

Features: The Dee Family Main Lobby was designed to create a healing environment and boasts a beautiful grand piano generously gifted by the Stewart Education Foundation. Space is both efficient and comfortable for patients and physicians in this area of the hospital.

This page: The double corridor and open hospital plan are efficiently organized to make it easy for patients and other visitors to find their way around. Every area of the hospital is well lighted, often naturally during the day from skylights. Corridors and waiting areas are enhanced with large framed paintings of a cheerful nature, well-manicured plants, and aquariums with colorful fish.

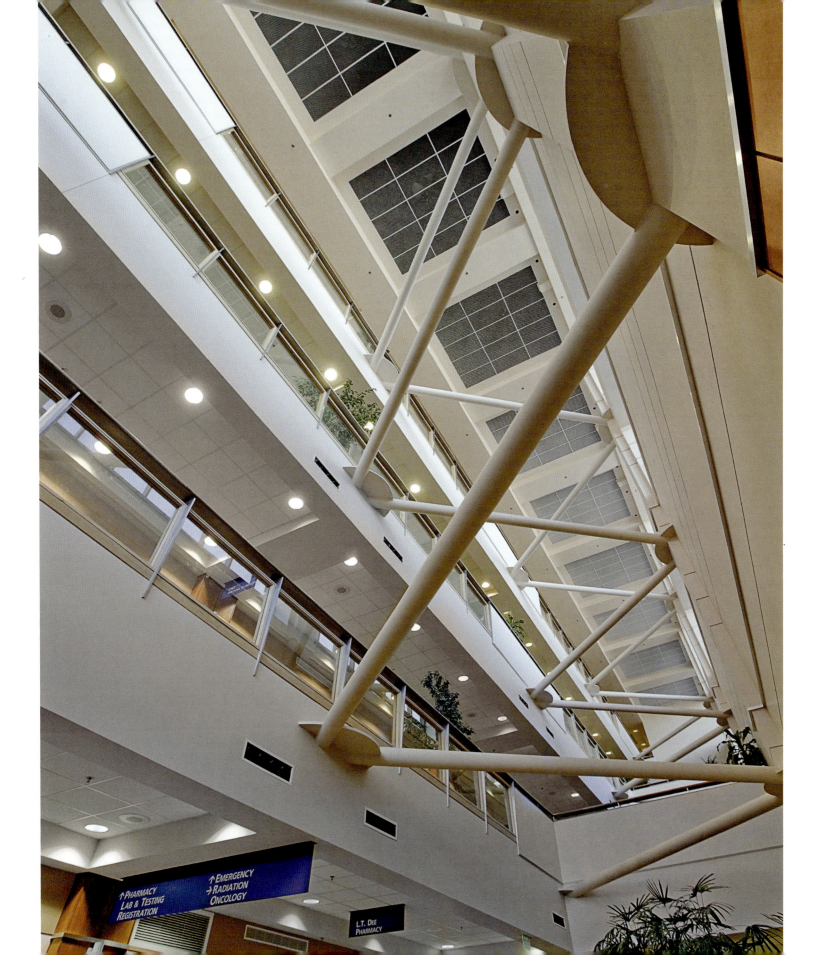

PHARMACY
LAB & TESTING
REGISTRATION

EMERGENCY
RADIATION
ONCOLOGY

L.T. DEE
PHARMACY

Separating the private corridor from parallel public areas allows patients to feel safe, comfortable, and at ease. Patients in hospital gowns appreciate feeling less exposed while moving to and from treatment areas or while doing their "recovery walks" following surgery in preparation for being released to go home. This essential passageway also allows physicians, nurses, and other caregivers to quickly and easily move equipment and supplies to their patients.

PATIENT-ROOM PLANNING FOR THE NEW HOSPITAL CENTER

John Grima, McKay-Dee's former Planning Director, says the new McKay-Dee Hospital Center's patient rooms are a great improvement over the former hospital's. "The big issue in the previous hospital was the narrow width of the rooms. Standards and technology have changed over time, and now healing work requires our medical professionals to be able to get equipment on both sides of a patient's bed. The hospital also wanted the ability to add and subtract monitors without having to rewire or restructure the building."

Today, patient rooms are zoned so the family can be in the room while the caregiver is working with the patient. A sink is available near the bed for the caregiver, as well as in the patient's bathroom. Space is also provided for an essential computer. The days of clipboard charts are long past. In a "paperless" hospital like McKay-Dee, nurses and doctors record the patient's vital signs, medications administered, treatments given, and so on right at the bedside. The information is then sent to nurses, doctors, and other professionals in every pertinent area of the hospital. Gone are the days of paper records stored somewhere in the basement. All patient data is electronically and securely archived for retrieval even years later if necessary.

The standard patient room is 320 square feet, including the bathroom, with dimensions that allow for visitors, caregivers, and equipment on both sides of the bed without anyone feeling cramped or in the way.

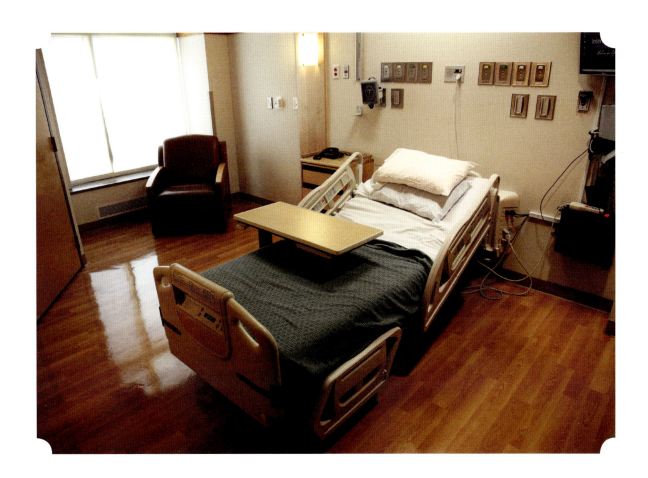

Fresh Air And Sun

Above: A mile-long fitness pathway marked at every quarter-mile traces the perimeter of the McKay-Dee Hospital Center's campus. Patients, employees, and the public use it year-round. McKay-Dee's landscaping includes colorful perennials and annuals planted seasonally.

Right: Patients, caregivers and visitors can sit and enjoy the parklike setting around the hospital campus.

Patients and their guests experience comfort — and often awe — while enjoying the breathtaking Great Salt Lake and Wasatch Front Mountain range from hospital lounge-area windows on several floors.

"Our Boys," a family gift in memory of Bill and Todd Miller, stands beside the reflecting pool and fountain on the south end of the hospital campus. The bronze piece by world-renowned sculptor Stanley J. Watts, a Salt Lake City native, was dedicated in October 2008. It depicts a happy time in the Miller boys' life. In 2005, at age 37, Todd died of brain cancer. Six months later, Bill, who had been a special needs child, died at age 28. He loved Superman and is seen wearing his superhero cape while "flying" in his Radio Flyer wagon being pulled by Todd.

In 2004, Tom Hanrahan, who had been CEO of McKay-Dee since 1986, was promoted to Regional Vice President of the Urban North Region of Intermountain Healthcare, responsible for McKay-Dee and Logan Regional hospitals. At that time, Tim Pehrson was named Administrator of McKay-Dee. When Hanrahan retired in 2008, Pehrson, who was already CEO of McKay-Dee, was promoted to also take on the position of Regional Vice President of the Urban North Region of Intermountain Healthcare. Regional duties were expanded at that time to include supervision of McKay-Dee, Logan Regional, and Bear River Valley hospitals.

FOOD AND NUTRITION SERVICES

In 2005, Food and Nutrition Services began an extensive research project to determine what patients thought of McKay-Dee Hospital food. Survey results indicated that only 22 percent of patients liked the food and that 40 percent of the food was wasted.

Guided by additional research, administrators determined that room service, enabling patients to order what they wanted when they felt like eating, would best serve patient needs and get patients back on the road to recovery more quickly.

Patients have a variety of dishes to choose from at times convenient for them. Menus include low-sodium and heart-healthy icons for easy identification and ordering when physicians restrict choices for cardiac and diabetic patients. Each selection on the menu shows the item's carbohydrate content in grams, ensuring healthy portions.

McKay-Dee's 100th anniversary menu includes grilled salmon, roasted turkey, chicken cordon bleu, fettuccine Alfredo, and cheese quesadillas. Yes, it is hospital food — prepared by McKay-Dee's staff of excellent chefs.

Since room service began in 2007 and food preparation was kicked up a notch, 80 percent of patients rate their meals as excellent or very good. Less food is wasted as well. The changes no doubt improve the patients' experience at the hospital.

Visitors to the hospital also enjoy the food prepared and served in the Mountain View Café and Grille. The restaurant, made possible by a generous gift from hospital employees, features indoor seating, as well as outdoor seating under a trellis or large umbrellas that provide shade while customers eat, relax, and enjoy the view — the reflecting pond and park-like landscaping.

Fun Facts

- 531,000 meals were served in the Mountain View Café and Grille in 2009.

- More than 180,000 room-service meals were prepared for patients in 2009.

- The Food and Nutrition Services department provides catering for hospital meetings and other events, such as the Dee Memorial School of Nursing's Alumni organization gatherings.

- The department catered more than 250,000 meals in 2009.

Right: Stephanie Nielsen prepares a food-service plate.

McKay-Dee Food and Nutrition Services is dedicated to providing nutritious, flavorful food that exceeds our patients' and customers' expectations. We accomplish this with a creative and skilled staff, a beautiful, clean facility, and a dedication to fresh ingredients and excellent service. Because patients are enjoying their food more and eating more of it, clinical outcomes have a higher likelihood of improvement as well.

—Kathleen Nielsen, Director of Food and Nutrition Services

This page: McKay-Dee Hospital's Mountain View Café and Grille offers a relaxing environment and a variety of dishes to choose from.

FULFILLING THE MISSION: PROVIDING QUALITY CARE

McKay-Dee Hospital is first and foremost committed to the provision of excellent healthcare. CEO Tim Pehrson explains, "To deliver on that promise, Intermountain Healthcare has created what are called Clinical Programs. The idea is built around organizing our doctors, nurses, and professional staff around improving clinical processes. For example, the Women and Newborn clinical program gathers OB/GYNs, perinatologists, neonatologists, pediatricians, nurses, respiratory therapists, statisticians, and management to proactively address clinical problems for women and infants. They look at evidence-based medical literature and ask how they can do better. They set goals and measure themselves on how they perform. This process helps caregivers become more consistent in their applications of best-practice protocols meant to keep the patient safe. We are seeing great results from our clinical programs and receiving national recognition for our efforts."

Annie Taylor Dee's generosity 100 years ago established the character of McKay-Dee Hospital. Pehrson says, "We provide the same dignified service and high-quality care to those in need, without regard to their ability to pay. Our goal is to provide compassionate, high-quality healthcare at the lowest appropriate cost. Our mission drives how we deliver that care."

Healers are the service groups who reach out — those doctors, nurses, volunteers, and other clinical professionals who work every day to provide the best care for patients, with clinical excellence, compassion, and understanding. Yet healers aren't only those who close wounds or deliver babies. At McKay-Dee Hospital Center, we believe all employees contribute to the healing process, whether they interact directly with patients or support those who do.

McKay-Dee's Newborn Intensive Care Unit

Every year, the McKay-Dee NICU treats about 650 babies, with a daily census of 25 to 30, says Robert D. Christensen, MD, director of Neonatology. The average stay is 20 days. Dr. Christensen is nationally recognized in his field for research focused on improving "preemie" care.

"About 11 percent of all births nationally occur in the NICU, primarily due to premature birth weight," says Dr. Christensen. "Most babies go home completely ready for approximately 85 years of productive living."

According to him, that's the best part of his job.

McKay-Dee's 32-bed NICU is top-rated. Mortality rates at McKay-Dee are lower than those in the 400 to 500 other hospitals in its comparable peer group worldwide, according to Dr. Christensen.

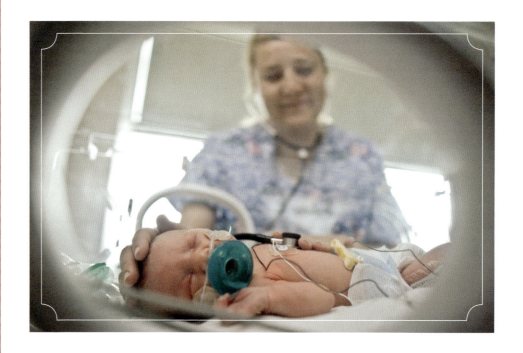

This page: Preemies and full-term newborns receive treatment in infant warmers and incubators. Many warmers are provided by McKay-Dee Hospital Foundation donors.

Facing: McKay-Dee's Level III NICU has 32 beds and includes a care team of neonatologists, nurse practitioners, and 100 registered nurses. Rounding out the team are respiratory therapists, social workers, and certified nursing assistants. A productive research program and the latest technology ensure extraordinary treatment for premature babies. McKay-Dee's Newborn Intensive Care Unit offers technology specifically for premature infants.

Nearly 4,500 babies are born each year at McKay-Dee Hospital. The hospital has 14 birthing suites, along with two adjacent surgical suites to accommodate cesarean delivery and postpartum surgical procedures.

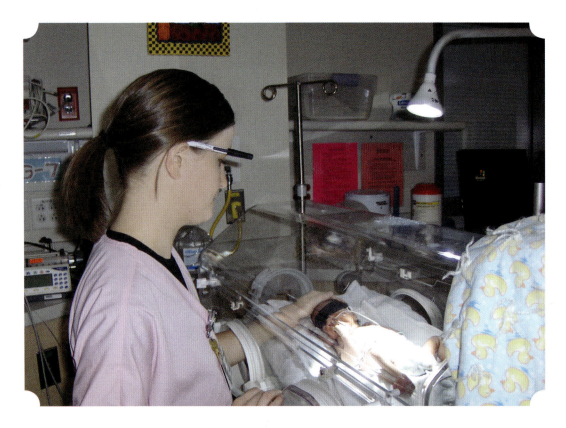

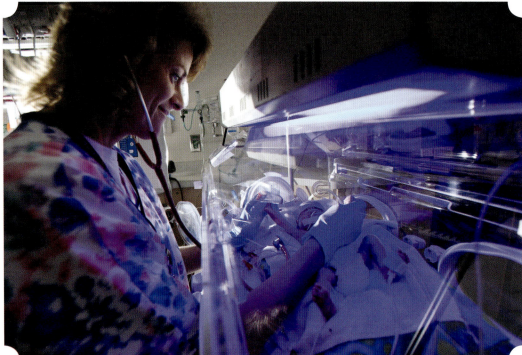

This page, top: Infant warmers purchased by McKay-Dee Hospital Foundation donors and given to the Newborn Intensive Care Unit of the Women and Newborns Department bring comfort to premature babies.

Left: The latest in light technology for preventing and alleviating jaundice in newborns is the Bilirubin, a blue-light tanning type of bed. This technology was provided by McKay-Dee Hospital Foundation donors.

Facing: McKay-Dee nurses are trained to care for each child with the utmost compassion and are committed to the child's welfare above all else. Casey Davis, a certified Child Life Specialist, comforts a newborn.

When a child is in the hospital, you're not just treating him or her; you're treating the whole family. You have to treat the needs of parents, too. We get a lot of joy out of making a difference in a child's life; it brings reward to our daily work.

—Neil Garner, Manager of Pediatric Services

Pediatrics Department

McKay-Dee's Pediatric Services Department treats children up to 18 years of age. There are 10 beds, sometimes expanding to 25 in winter months, when there tends to be more children with respiratory infections.

Neil Garner, Manager of Pediatric Services for the hospital, reminisces about changes he has seen over the years.

"I remember Dr. Wilson Hales. He would line up children and meet with them the night before their tonsillectomies. He would explain to all of them what was going to happen with surgery the following day and then send them home for a good night's rest."

Parents were not allowed to stay in the large wardrooms with their children, but now parents can stay in their child's private room.

From left: Melanie Williams, Support Partner-Administrative; Neil Garner, Manager of Pediatric Services; and Danielle Nef, RN, work in the Pediatrics Department, which treats children up to age 18.

During flu season, 10 pediatric patients may be admitted within a matter of just a few hours. Julie Talbot, RN, helps a young patient color a picture.

The Dr. Ezekiel R. and Edna Wattis Dumke Surgical Unit

A full spectrum of surgical specialists practices at McKay-Dee, including those in the specialties of: ears, nose and throat; dental; heart; cancer; orthopedics; podiatry; plastic/cosmetic surgery; gynecology; ophthalmology; urology; neurosurgery; and general surgery.

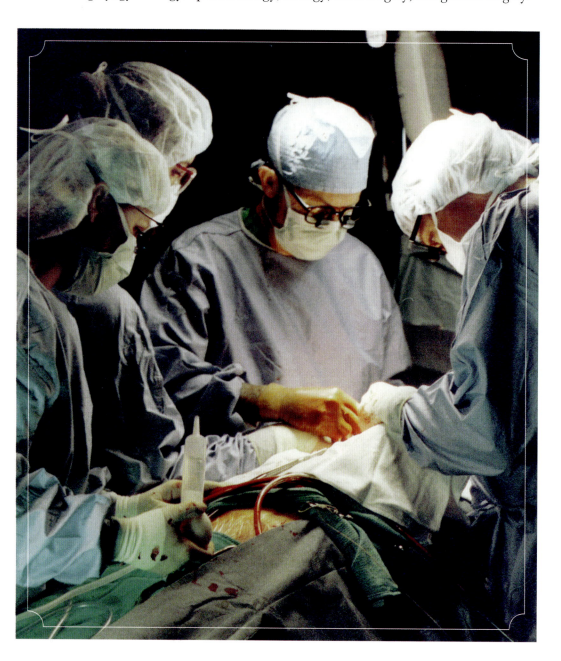

McKay-Dee Hospital specializes in a wide variety of surgical procedures and strives to update equipment as technology advances.

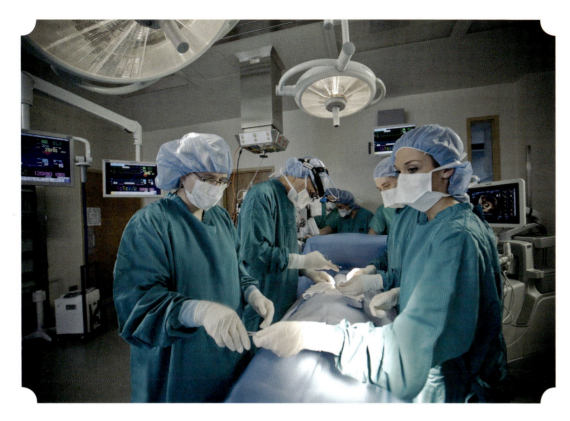

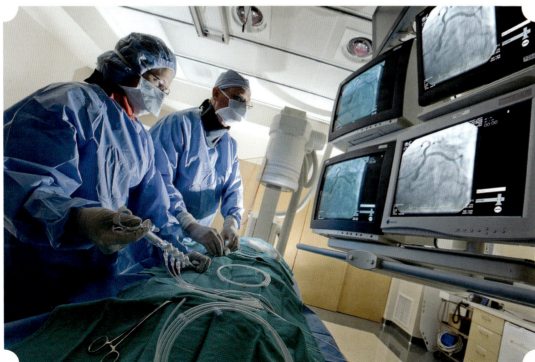

This page: McKay-Dee Hospital's technological improvements include the latest in noninvasive imaging procedures.

THE STEWART NEUROLOGICAL, ORTHOPEDIC, AND REHABILITATION UNIT

From beginnings at McKay-Dee Hospital in 1974, Stewart Rehab Services has expanded to include four additional clinics in Davis and Weber counties. They offer treatment to patients of all ages seeking a comprehensive range of specialized services.

Inpatient Services

Located on the second floor of the hospital, Inpatient Rehab provides expert, specialized care within a state-of-the-art facility. Serving patients with a variety of diagnoses including stroke, orthopedic, spinal cord, and traumatic brain injuries, Stewart Rehab is staffed by highly skilled physical, occupational, and speech therapists.

Outpatient Services

McKay-Dee Stewart Rehab Center is a large, multidisciplinary center of excellence offering orthopedics, neurological rehabilitation, balance, pediatric rehab, wound, ostomy, and lymphedema services.

Sports Medicine and Orthopedic Services

From sports injuries to joint replacements, recovery takes time. Age and health condition of the patient are important aspects of healing. Stewart Rehab Center's Sports Medicine and Orthopedic Services is staffed by the area's most experienced therapists to get the patient one step closer to returning to normal daily activities. Since 2008, McKay-Dee has been the official provider for the U.S. Ski and Snowboard Association, providing therapists and trainers who travel throughout the world during competition.

Other Services

Stewart Rehab offers programs for healthy and active lifestyles, including Bike Fit Test, pilates and yoga classes, no-charge injury assessments, and a return-to-driving program.

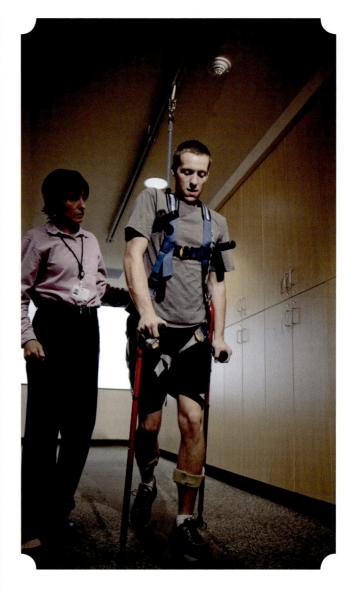

This page: Since 2007, when Stewart Rehab Services was revamped, outpatient services for those needing muscle, bone, and nerve "retraining" as they recovered mobility after injury or surgery were transferred to the Stewart Rehabilitation fourth floor on the North Campus. Financial support provided by the Mary Elizabeth Dee Shaw Foundation made the new outpatient services possible.

Facing: JoAnn Yngsdal, Physical Therapist, enjoys working with a patient.

Facing, inset: Dontai Warner, Patient Care Assistant, helps a patient work toward recovery.

Stewart Rehab Center
Hand and Voice / Ogden

•

Stewart Rehab Center
Layton Clinic

•

Stewart Rehab Center
North Ogden Clinic

•

Stewart Rehab Center
West Ogden Clinic

THE VAL AND ANN BROWNING CANCER CENTER

The opening of the new McKay-Dee Hospital set the stage for a truly integrated and comprehensive cancer program with Radiation Therapy, Medical Oncology (chemotherapy), and Surgical Services together under one roof. Before the Cancer Services program was created, many patients had to be referred to other facilities. Today, oncology services at McKay-Dee Hospital Center include:

• Multidisciplinary cancer clinics
• Treatment and coordination of service needs
• Comprehensive education and resources

Resources also include outstanding oncology social work, and rehabilitation, pathology, radiology, women's imaging services, and a cancer registry.

The hospital also offers a no-cost cancer support group for those fighting cancer, as well as for the adult family members who support them. The group meets twice a month, covering such topics as coping skills, handling children's grief, dealing with pain, and more. It also provides educational materials and a place to talk with others facing the same issues.

McKay-Dee's medical oncology group leads the state and much of the nation in clinical-trial enrollments and participation in the latest studies.

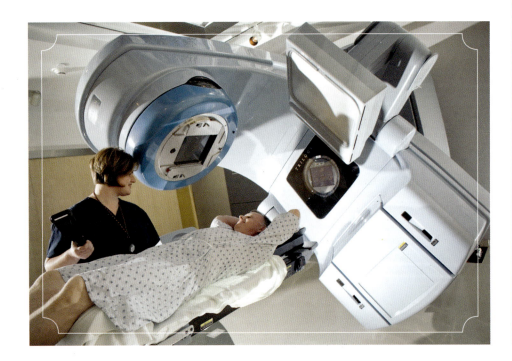

This Linear Accelerator at the Val and Ann Browning Cancer Center was made possible by a generous gift from the Browning family and other community donors.

Cancer Rehabilitation at the Cardiac Fitness Institute of McKay-Dee Hospital

The institute is designed to help patients improve their quality of life. The cancer exercise program benefits patients with a cancer diagnosis during and after treatment who are seeking:

- *Improved range of motion*
- *Reduced fatigue, nausea, and other treatment-related side effects*
- *Improved functional ability*
- *Improved ability to maintain body weight*
- *Enhanced body image*
- *Enhanced sense of control*
- *Improved mood and quality of life*

The Cardiac Fitness Institute at McKay-Dee Hospital Center is accredited by the American Association of Cardiovascular and Pulmonary Rehab. The institute is recognized by the American College of Sports Medicine as one of only a handful of facilities nationally with 85 percent of the staff having achieved the Gold Standard Certification of Clinical Exercise Specialist. Educational components include: smoking cessation, healthy eating, stress management, and exercise.

Julie Brandt, Exercise Physiologist II, helps patient Donna Christensen with strength training.

Dan Beatty exercises under the watchful eye of Melanie Egbert, an Exercise Physiologist in the Cardiac Fitness Center.

Over the last several years, I have had the opportunity to make a career of caring for the needs of cancer patients and their families. In no other place I've worked has there been such a caring, dedicated, and effective group of people. McKay-Dee Hospital is a place where the hopes and dreams of people working to find a cure for cancer come alive.

—J. Paul Weight, MBA, RTT,
Cancer Services Director/Manager Radiation Therapy

THE GEORGE S. AND DOLORES DORÉ ECCLES HEART INSTITUTE

McKay-Dee was recognized as one of the "Top 100 Heart Hospitals in 2006" by the Solucient research firm and Modern Healthcare magazine. Garry W. MacKenzie, MD, head of Cardiology and chief of Cardiovascular Medicine and Surgery at McKay-Dee, is proud to say, "Our excellent systems here in cardiovascular service lines are a result of the hospital's early focus on improving outcomes. Our clinical program efforts help us improve by studying outcomes and figuring out what we can do better. I've never seen that in any other hospital where I've worked in the U.S. or Canada."

Below, left: Julie Burchell, MS, RN, is the Continuum Care Manager of the Heart Failure Clinic.

Inset: Each year, 228 cardiac patients clutch heart-shaped pillows to their chests when coughing or practicing deep-breathing exercises after valve or bypass surgery. This exercise helps prevent pneumonia and keeps airways open, but it's also painful because of the new incision area. Hugging the pillow eases the patients' pain while protecting the incision. The McKay-Dee Hospital Foundation and its donors make these pillows available for patients receiving surgical heart services.

> *We focus on providing first-class technology in diagnostic and treatment equipment, as well as programs, in this beautiful, clean, and efficient facility. The standard of healthcare here is outstanding, due in great part to the quality of the medical professionals.*
>
> *—Dr. Garry W. MacKenzie, cardiologist and chief of the Department of Cardiovascular Medicine and Surgery*

Sam Banner, of Brigham City, and his son Todd, of South Weber, were acting as volunteer patients for a publicity TV commercial at McKay-Dee Hospital with Dr. Garry MacKenzie, cardiologist and chief of the hospital's Department of Cardiovascular Medicine and Surgery. To make the situation comfortable, Dr. MacKenzie asked the Banners questions about their health and hearts. Recognizing immediately that Sam was experiencing classic symptoms of unstable angina, Dr. MacKenzie arranged to have him tested the next day. A few days later, Sam Banner underwent successful quadruple bypass surgery. Commenting on Sam Banner and many other patients, Dr. MacKenzie said, "Most people experience warning symptoms before having a major heart problem, but they often disregard those warnings." Fortunately for Sam Banner, his condition was diagnosed in time, and the outcomes were positive, enhancing his quality of life.

Melanie Egbert, Exercise Physiologist, works with patient Alvin Carter.

Life Flight, Emergency Response Mobile Intensive Care Unit

Since the new McKay-Dee Hospital opened in 2002, it has served as Intermountain Healthcare's Life Flight Northern Utah base of operations. Life Flight provides faster service and better care for patients who need a mobile intensive care unit. Since its inception, Life Flight has grown in scope of services, technology, medical personnel, and in actual numbers of air-service vehicles. In addition to the thousands of flights transporting emergency patients, Life Flight teams have conducted more than 100 rescue missions in difficult-to-reach areas. For more than 25 years, medical professionals for Life Flight Children's Services have provided ongoing collaborative education and training in neonatal management to hospital and pre-hospital healthcare professionals throughout the local community and beyond. Additionally, they provide training and education to many of their national and international colleagues at the critically acclaimed annual Current Concepts in Transport conference.

Above: Rose Linsler, RN, Life Flight II Pediatric, and Jim Zobell, RN, Life Flight II, reassure a patient needing Life Flight transport.

Facing, top, left: Life Flight Pilot Earl Jewkes sometimes must fly dangerous missions into difficult-to-reach areas.

Facing, bottom left: With outdoor recreation so popular in Utah, Life Flight crews must sometimes risk their lives to rescue people who have become injured in the backcountry.

Life Flight by the Numbers in 2010

270 full- and part-time professionals, including nurses, pilots, and administrative staff throughout Utah

50 full- and part-time Life Flight team members at McKay-Dee Hospital Center

12 transport flights on average per day, available 24/7, for a total of 4,380 flights per year

In 2005, the Emergency Department was expanded to add five new exam rooms, a staff lounge, coding and billing workspaces, charting and storage areas, and consulting and emergency supplies areas. A gift by the Mary Elizabeth Dee Shaw Foundation made the expansion possible.

Officer Matt Gailey and canine Dax are on duty in the Emergency Department on weekend nights, when people who have abused alcohol or drugs are more likely to be brought in for urgent care.

THE WILLARD AND RUTH ECCLES EMERGENCY SERVICES DEPARTMENT

On average, more than 65,000 individuals are treated each year at McKay-Dee Hospital's Emergency Department. And most of the patients admitted, excluding maternity, come through the ER. Three years after opening, in 2005, expansion was necessary. Dr. Richard Arbogast, chief of the Medical Staff, said, "Until Intermountain Medical Center in Murray, Utah, opened in 2008, McKay-Dee Hospital Center had the highest volume ED in the state. Amazingly, this tremendous volume doesn't inconvenience patients. On average, patients see an ED doctor within 30 minutes of arrival."

Additionally, McKay-Dee Hospital Center is designated a Level 2 Trauma Center, an impressive rating for a community hospital. In 2007, the Joint Commission, a national hospital accrediting body, certified McKay-Dee Hospital Center as a Primary Stroke Center.

Emergency Department Services

Trauma Bays

The hospital has three trauma bays for highly critical patients. These rooms have direct entry from the ambulance dock and are equipped comparably to an operating room. A Fast Track area is also available for patients with less severe conditions. It is staffed by a dedicated physician 12 to 16 hours a day during the busiest times in order to facilitate quick-in, quick-out treatment.

Clinical Decision Unit

The observation area is primarily used for cardiac patients when the emergency team is not certain whether the patient is experiencing cardiac symptoms or something else. The patient is kept in this unit until a clear diagnosis can be made and the patient is released to go home or admitted to the hospital for further treatment.

The professional teams in McKay–Dee Hospital Center's emergency and critical care units are committed to helping the sickest and the most vulnerable. Every patient receives the best assessment and treatment available anywhere, regardless of their ability to pay.

—*Kayleen Paul, RN, Director, Emergency, Critical Care, and Trauma Services*

ICU Nursing Coordinator Marra Lane, Paul B. Kim, MD, and RN, Edie Burt, work together so patients needing critical care get the best treatment possible.

BEHAVIORAL HEALTH

Dating back to the Dee Hospital, which had an adult psychiatric unit, behavioral health professionals at McKay-Dee have continued to work to ensure evidence-based quality care. Board certified psychiatrists, psychologists, psychiatric nurse practitioners, licensed clinical social workers, licensed professional counselors, and other providers bring a team approach to the discipline of behavioral health. The result is more compassionate patient support. Behavioral Health Services is on the first floor of the Patient Tower near the Emergency Department and provides inpatient, outpatient, and day-treatment programs for adults and adolescents. Based on patient needs, the service line has continued to grow. In June 2009, 12 beds were added to the adult inpatient unit to accommodate growing patient demand.

Behavioral Health Institute

McKay-Dee's Behavioral Health Institute is located at 5030 Harrison Boulevard and opened in 1987. Services include:

- *16-bed inpatient unit for patients ages 15–17*
- *Summit Family-Centered Day Treatment Unit for patients ages 12–18*
- *Outpatient Services include psychiatrists, advanced practice registered nurses, psychologists, and therapists*

At McKay-Dee Hospital's Behavioral Health Services, the well-being of the patient's body, mind, and spirit is the paramount concern.

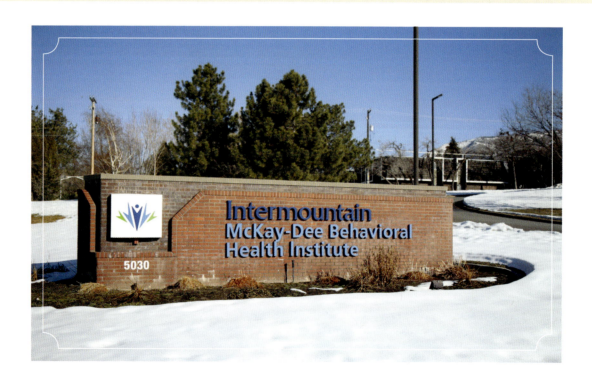

Dee to McKay-Dee to Intermountain McKay-Dee Hospital Center Employees

Amazingly enough, Intermountain McKay-Dee Hospital Center has employees who have made the transition from facility, to facility, to facility! The following employees share an impressive legacy of service from the original facility, Thomas D. Dee Memorial Hospital, to the McKay-Dee Hospital at 3939 Harrison Boulevard, and finally to today's modern Intermountain McKay-Dee Hospital Center at 4401 Harrison Boulevard. The hospital salutes the following people, listed with their hire date. Some may have served in the original Dee Hospital as interns or students and begun working at the hospital after raising their families.

Kathy Adams – *Risk Management* / 1972 *(Student at Dee)*
Elwyn Bodily – *Operating Rooms* / 1968
Connie Bohman – *Quality Management* / 1981
Yvonne Bouwhis – *Women's Clinic* / 1971
Marilyn Clarke – *Radiology* / 1978
Sandra Dahl – *Labor and Delivery* / 1965
Patty Flint – *Same-Day Surgery* / 1986
Carol Godfrey – *Cardiovascular Thoracic* / 1966
Leilani Grange – *Laboratory* / 1966
Joann Hackley – *Psychiatry* / 1967
Carl Hamilton – *Radiology* / 1966
Leota Ito – *Community Health Information* / 1980
Vernon Johnson – *Plant Operations* / 1969
Joan Lindley – *Same-Day Surgery* / 1972
Patricia J. Lindsay – *Operating Rooms* / 1990
Dianne Montgomery – *Neonatology* / 1982
Pieter Oenes – *Materials Management* / 1962
Kayleen Paul – *Emergency, Critical Care & Trauma* / 1975
Verlene Scott – *Maternal Fetal Medicine* / 1966
Marvin Shaw – *Plant Operations* / 1968

Frank Southwick – *Plant Operations* / 1976
Verona Strong – *Maternal Fetal Medicine* / 1969
Linda Thorsted – *Laboratory* / 1969
David Vandenbosch – *Laboratory* / 1968
Sally Whitehead – *CV Medical Oncology Administration* / 1967
Jill Whiteley – *Operating Rooms* / 1966
Barbara Williams – *Women's Clinic* / 1967
Diane Woolsey – *McKay-Dee Surgical Center* / 1966

Ogden's newest hospital facility has provided care to thousands of patients since it opened at 4401 Harrison Boulevard in 2002. The Intermountain Healthcare system member continues to strive for high-quality patient care — both physically, mentally and emotionally.

Since Anne Taylor Dee brought her dream of quality healthcare in Ogden to fruition in 1910, residents of Ogden and the surrounding communities — Northern Utah, Southern Idaho and Western Wyoming — have worked to help the hospital technologically advance by financially contributing in support of the wellness of the whole person.

Intermountain McKay-Dee Hospital Center has become a vital part of many people's lives — as a workplace, a wellness center, an acute-care facility, a place of recovery, and as a volunteer opportunity. Those endeavors are sure to endure as nearby communities grow, technology advances, and both the medical field and patients continue their focus on the wellness of mind, body, and spirit. ❧

Our Commitment
to a Healing Experience

*As an Intermountain Healthcare employee, I am committed
to creating an extraordinary experience for those I serve.*

I help you feel safe, welcome and at ease.

I listen to you with sensitivity and
respond to your needs.

I treat you with respect and compassion.

I keep you informed and involved.

I ensure our team works with you.

I take responsibility to help solve problems.

PART TWO

100 YEARS of HOSPITAL CARING and SERVICE

People Make *All* the *Difference*

WHEN OGDEN WAS FIRST SETTLED, MANY PRACTICING MEDICINE WERE BOTANISTS, MIDWIVES WHO RELIED ON HERBS, FOLKLORE, AND EXPERIENCE, OR MEDICINE SHOW DOCTORS WHO SKEDADDLED OUT OF TOWN BEFORE THEIR CUSTOMERS COULD FIGURE OUT THEY'D BEEN SCAMMED INTO SPENDING THEIR HARD-EARNED MONEY ON WORTHLESS REMEDIES. FORMAL MEDICAL TRAINING WAS PRACTICALLY UNHEARD OF IN THE 1880S.

Ogden's need for medical care and hospital services became acute when the railroad was established, making Junction City more susceptible to smallpox, diphtheria, scarlet fever, and typhoid fever, according to "*Weber County's History*," by Richard W. Sadler and Richard C. Roberts. The closest thing the area had to a hospital was a hotel where rooms for the most serious cases were set aside so it was easier for the area's few true physicians to care for patients.

In 1882, an isolation facility was built in Ogden for the care of patients with contagious diseases that were potentially fatal. The next year, the Union Pacific Railroad Company purchased an existing building in town and used it to treat railroad workers until 1897, according to "*Weber County's History*."

Ogden built a hospital in 1892 for $25,000, but the facility closed a year later. It wasn't until 1897 that it was reopened by a group of Weber County doctors who leased the building and remodeled it. However, the structure had only six or eight private rooms, in addition to a surgical ward and operating rooms, and care cost so much that few average citizens could afford treatment. Nurses learned on the job in this facility until it closed in 1910, when the Thomas D. Dee Memorial Hospital opened and medical care in Ogden was changed forever.

Starting around 1896, medical school attendance of two to three years was required of those wanting to be licensed physicians, so the Dee opened with doctors who'd been educated in the medical field. The hospital also made patient care more affordable. Founder Annie Taylor Dee even paid for the care of women who would agree to give birth in the hospital so the Dee's nurses could receive training in labor and delivery.

Annie was determined that patients at the Dee would receive top-notch care, and that required nurses with more than hands-on training. It is thanks to her that nursing education became so prominent and patients were tenderly cared for by nurses who received instruction by physicians and were put through

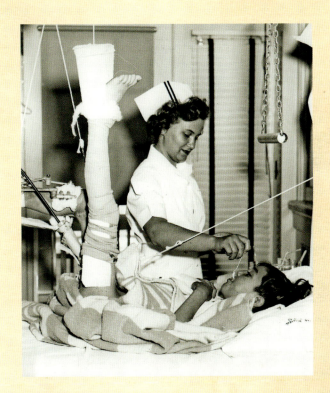

rigorous training in all areas of the hospital.

Thomas D. Dee Memorial Hospital may have changed locations and names — becoming McKay-Dee Hospital at 3939 Harrison Boulevard in 1969 and Intermountain McKay-Dee Hospital Center at 4401 Harrison Boulevard in 2002 — but some things never change. The determination to value and fulfill the mission of Annie Taylor Dee continues today.

Thanks to the perseverance and generosity of the LDS Church, hospital administrators, boards of trustees, medical chiefs, physicians, nurses and other hospital staff, as well as volunteers and financial donors too numerous to count, Annie's dream is still alive and Ogden is home to many options for wellness, recovery, and the health of body, mind, and spirit. ◂

LEADING THE WAY THROUGH THE DECADES

Every major undertaking needs leaders — people to build the foundation, set the standards, be the cheerleaders, rouse supporters, and plan for the future.

Throughout the hospital's history — from the Dee in 1910 to McKay-Dee in 1969 to Intermountain McKay-Dee in 2002 and today — people have stepped up in various capacities to ensure the continued quality of medical care. Many have contributed to the realization of Anne Taylor Dee's dream by having open minds, a willingness to hear and adopt new ideas, the drive to seek excellent models from around the world, the character to place quality above quantity and people over money, and the understanding that wellness hinges on treating body, mind, and spirit.

Those who have stepped up and devoted their endeavors to helping others have made McKay-Dee the hospital it is today. It is their dedication that has made the hospital an icon in the community and set the tone for the future of healthcare in Ogden, the surrounding areas, and across the United States.

HOSPITAL ADMINISTRATORS SET THE TONE

Whether the position was called "steward," "superintendent," "administrator," or "CEO," the role of the Dee and McKay-Dee's chief executive has remained essentially the same: to facilitate the acquisition of land, structures, equipment, and staff needed to provide excellent healthcare.

Ten administrators have led the hospital over its 100 years. They have provided an enduring legacy of extraordinary, leading healthcare and set the tone for those working and volunteering in the hospital. Their leadership has driven how healthcare is delivered, pushed hospital staff to strive for excellence, embraced new technology and procedures that keep the hospital in the public eye as a model for high-quality healthcare, and reassured patients that they will be treated with dignity and respect while staff handle medical issues to the best of their ability.

In its 100th anniversary year, McKay-Dee pays tribute to those administrators who have made the facility one of the best and most respected in the nation.

Little is known about those who were administrators early in the life of the hospital, but that does not lessen their impact. R.C. Lundy (1910 to 1915), O.J. Stilwell (1915 to 1916), Wilfred Rawson (1917 to 1933), Howard Jenkins (1933 to 1941), and Lawrence Evans (1941 to 1951) set the hospital on its course of excellence and compassion.

The administrators who followed continued where they left off, carrying on the values and mission of the hospital's original founders.

Kenneth E. Knapp
1951–1972

Ken Knapp was recruited to hospital administration out of the airline industry. He studied Hospital Administration at Northwestern University in Chicago and interned at two major hospitals before being appointed administrator of the Dee Hospital in 1951. He led efforts to build what became McKay-Dee Hospital at 3939 Harrison Boulevard.

Kenneth C. Johnson
1972–1980

In 1972, Ken Johnson was named administrator at McKay-Dee after service at Primary Children's Medical Center in Salt Lake City. He has degrees from Weber State College, University of Utah, and University of Minnesota. He became regional administrator for six Intermountain Healthcare hospitals in 1980. He went on to serve as a corporate vice president over all of Intermountain's hospitals.

H. Gary Pehrson
1980–1986

Gary Pehrson started at McKay-Dee as assistant administrator in 1972. Prior to that, he had held assistant administrator positions at McKay-Dee, Pocatello Regional, and Primary Children's. In 1985, he became vice president of the Northern Region for Intermountain Healthcare. He went on to serve in the same position in the Urban Central Region in Salt Lake City, where he led efforts to build the Intermountain Medical Center. He holds degrees from the University of Utah and UCLA.

Thomas F. Hanrahan
1986–2004

Prior to coming to McKay-Dee in 1983, Tom Hanrahan held administrative positions at hospitals in Miami, Fla., and Mobile, Ala. He was educated at Marian College and Indiana University. He was named CEO of McKay-Dee in 1986 and vice president of the Urban North Region in 2004. He led efforts to build the new Intermountain McKay-Dee Hospital Center at 4401 Harrison Boulevard.

Timothy T. Pehrson
2004–Present

Tim Pehrson, the CEO of McKay-Dee Hospital and the CEO and vice president of Intermountain Healthcare's North Region, is responsible for McKay-Dee, Logan Regional, and Bear River Valley hospitals. In 2000, he came to McKay-Dee, where he worked as an assistant administrator until being named administrator in 2004. A graduate of Brigham Young University and the University of Michigan, he worked in Arizona before coming to McKay-Dee.

BOARD OF TRUSTEES THROUGH THE YEARS

The Board of Trustees works behind the scenes to manage hospital affairs and sometimes make difficult decisions essential to the survival of a vital community asset.

Annie Taylor Dee, who founded the Thomas D. Dee Memorial Hospital in 1910, was the first to lead the hospital's Board of Trustees. With her guidance, the board oversaw a fledgling facility and, when financial difficulties loomed in 1915, entrusted the LDS Church with carrying the hospital forward. In 1970, the hospital was to still be owned and operated by the Church, but its Board of Trustees would begin reporting to a central board under the control of the new Health Services Corporation, allowing the Church to devote its attention to other efforts.

In 1974, the Church gave its 15 hospitals back to their communities, and a newly formed, not-for-profit corporation, Intermountain Healthcare, would ensure the hospitals would continue as community assets, providing charity care when needed.

The Board of Trustees has helped the hospital — as the Dee, McKay-Dee, and Intermountain McKay-Dee — remain true to its mission of providing quality care — charity and otherwise — through these ownership and control changes, as well as technological and site changes. Today, the hospital remembers with appreciation those who have provided stability and enthusiasm while leading the Board through the last century.

Those who followed in Annie Taylor Dee's footsteps as chair of the Board are:

Henry J. Rolapp	1916-1917
W.H. Wattis	1917-1929
Sylvester Q. Cannon	1929-1938
LeGrande Richards	1938-1958
Thorpe B. Isaacson	1958-1962
John H. Vandenberg	1962-1969
Albert L. Bott	1970-1972
Nathan C. Tanner	1972-1982
Paul T. Kunz	1982-2002
E. Rich Brewer	2002-2005
Edward G. Kleyn	2005-2008
Karen Fairbanks	2008-present

The medical staff of the Dee Hospital posed for this photograph in 1937.

Guiding the Medical Staff

Even before the Dee was founded, a physician was playing a key role in what would evolve into one of the leading hospitals in the country. When Annie Taylor Dee was mourning her husband and wondering how to best honor his memory, she sought advice from Dr. Robert S. Joyce, a railroad physician who had become like a son to her and her husband. Dr. Joyce encouraged her to establish a facility specifically for providing acute care to residents of Ogden and the towns growing nearby.

Dr. Joyce was a member of the Dee's very first Board of Trustees and became the first chief of staff, directing the hospital's first 30 or so physicians.

Over the years, the president of the medical staff oversaw advances in technology, updates in procedures, and the moves into new quarters — or new buildings altogether.

In its 100th year, McKay-Dee acknowledges the leadership of those who set examples of excellence for those providing medical care at the hospital.

Medical Staff Presidents

Donald Moore	(Medicine)	1953
R.L. Draper	(Family Practice)	1954
Anthony Lund	(Surgery)	1955
Drew Petersen	(Medicine)	1956
Russell Hirst	(Electrophysiology)	1957
W.H. Anderson	(Pediatrics)	1958
Dean Tanner	(Surgery)	1959
Rich Johnston	(Family Practice)	1960
W.J. Thomson	(Family Practice)	1961
Vernal Johnson	(OB/GYN)	1962
William Daines	(Medicine)	1963
Bruce Balken	(Pediatrics)	1964
Charles Pennington	(Family Practice)	1965
Rulon Howe	(Surgery)	1966
Thomas Feeny	(OB/GYN)	1967
Paul Southwick	(Medicine)	1968
Joe Amano	(Family Practice)	1969
Homer Rich	(Pediatrics)	1970
Boyd Farr	(OB/GYN)	1971
Harvey Wheelwright	(Psychiatry)	1972
LaVal Spencer	(Family Practice)	1973
Marvin Lewis	(Medicine)	1974
Winn Richards	(Surgery)	1975
Wendell Hyde	(Family Practice)	1976
Ralph Macfarlane	(Surgery)	1977
Basil Williams	(Medicine)	1978
Leon White	(Pediatrics)	1979
Merrill Godfrey	(OB/GYN)	1980
Marlan Haslam	(Surgery)	1981
David Jahsman	(Medicine)	1982
Richard White	(Medicine)	1983
Lyle Archibald	(Surgery)	1984
Phillip Hale	(Surgery)	1985
Floyd Seager	(Medicine)	1986
Darrell Woods	(OB/GYN)	1987
Richard Alder	(Surgery)	1988
Jeffrey Booth	(Medicine)	1989
Ernest Grua	(Surgery)	1990
Tom Blanch	(Medicine)	1991
Brent Wallace	(Family Practice)	1992
Darrell Dixon	(Family Practice)	1993
Robert Brodstein	(Surgery)	1994
David Carlquist	(Emergency Medicine)	1995
John Lowe	(Medicine)	1996-1997
Ray Yaworsky	(Pathology)	1998-1999
Steve Cain	(Cardiovascular Medicine Surgery)	2000-2001
Stewart Barlow	(Surgery)	2002-2003
Harry Senekjian	(Medicine)	2004-2007
Harold Vonk	(Medicine)	2007-2009
Garry MacKenzie	(Cardiology)	2009-present

BUILDING BLOCKS *of* MEDICAL CARE

A PHYSICIAN IS MORE THAN A PERSON KNOWLEDGEABLE ABOUT THE PROCESSES OF THE BODY AND HOW TO CORRECT ABNORMALITIES. A PHYSICIAN KNOWS HOW TO LISTEN TO A PATIENT'S DESCRIPTIONS OF SYMPTOMS AND FEELINGS. A PHYSICIAN STRIVES TO KEEP UP WITH ADVANCES IN TECHNOLOGY AND SCIENCE. A PHYSICIAN CARES ABOUT THE QUALITY OF CARE — NOT THE QUANTITY OF CARE.

A physician puts the needs of patients first and supports others providing care, including family members, nurses, therapists, specialists, X-ray and laboratory technicians, and all others on the rungs of the ladder to wellness.

Intermountain Healthcare and McKay-Dee strive to recruit and retain physicians and support staff who meet or exceed patients' expectations and needs. It is paramount that patients and other visitors to the hospital feel they receive the best care — both physical and emotional — during a stressful time. "Healing for Life" is deeply ingrained in the McKay-Dee culture of caring that reaches back to the hospital's founding.

TRAINING FOR EXCELLENT PRIMARY HEALTHCARE

In order to provide training for interns, an outpatient clinic was established in the south wing of the Dee in 1948. The next year, Maude Dee Porter provided funding to enlarge this section of the hospital and established the R.B. Porter Memorial Clinic in honor of her husband.

McKay-Dee's first class of family practice residents. *Back row from left:* Dr. Jerry Gardner, Dr. James Allred, and Dr. James Jacks. *Front row from left:* Dr. Kenneth Murdock, Dr. Boyd Hale, and Dr. Richard Wuthrich.

For many years, the Porter Family Clinic continued to supply training opportunities for interns, but it wasn't until July 1, 1971, that Utah's first family practice residency program was established at McKay-Dee Hospital Center with six physician residents.

George F. Snell, a family practitioner from Kaysville, directed the program. Its implementation was accomplished under the direction of the Department of Community and Family Medicine at the University of Utah School of Medicine in Salt Lake City.

For a doctor in training, residency is a time for gaining valuable clinical experience and interpersonal skills under the supervision of many doctors in a variety of settings before going into practice. Each new resident was assigned to a hospital physician who served as a primary contact during the three-year training period. Residents rotated through the clinical areas of the hospital, beginning on the medical and pediatric floors. The residents gained experience in all phases of care normally provided by a family physician, including chronic and acute illnesses, periodic health checkups, prenatal and postnatal care, office surgery, and treatment of emergency illnesses and injuries.

In 1980, McKay-Dee's family practice residency program was ranked in the nation's Top 10. McKay-Dee Hospital Center continues to provide an exemplary family practice residency program and had graduated 219 physicians through June 2009.

Today, the Porter Family Clinic continues to be a primary care practice setting for teaching the skills and demeanor needed to care for families. The clinic focuses on serving patients despite their ability to pay and was named as being in the top 10 percent of primary care clinics across the state in 2008 for both breast cancer and cervical cancer screenings.

The clinic benefits Intermountain Healthcare and the Top of Utah in another way as well. Many resident physicians from all over the country come to love Utah and its people so much that they establish their practices here, serving residents of the community for many years.

MEDICAL GROUP PHYSICIANS

Intermountain's McKay-Dee Hospital Center has long been at the forefront of providing cutting-edge medical care to the community. The same can be said of the hospital's relationship with physician clinics and practices.

McKay-Dee's medical staff has grown over the years to keep pace with the growing population and changing healthcare needs in 2010. The active medical staff is comprised of about 443 members, of which Intermountain Healthcare employs approximately 115 to work at McKay-Dee or in one of the Intermountain Healthcare clinics. The remainder of the staff, more than 300 physicians, continue to practice in more traditional models, individual practices, and small groups or as a member of a multispecialty clinic. All members of the staff participate fully in hospital activities, including a wide range of clinical programs and quality-improvement activities. Each member of the medical staff belongs to one of nine clinical departments, each of which has an elected physician leader who shares the responsibility with the hospital's Board of Trustees for the quality of evidence-based patient care.

In the early 1990s, McKay-Dee brought on a few family-practice groups, including Ogden Family Medicine, Herefordshire Clinic in Roy, and Fairfield Clinic in Layton. One of the physicians formerly of the Herefordshire Clinic is Brent E. Wallace, MD, current chief medical officer of Intermountain Healthcare. Wallace recalls that, at the time, he felt the future of medicine was going to be working with hospital systems and not just with independent practitioners because care and evidence-based medicine would improve if physicians and hospitals worked together more closely. "In 1990, I led our group to change and actually sell our practice. We were the first physicians not in a rural area to become employed by a hospital in the Intermountain area."

Through its residency program, McKay-Dee opened an urgent care clinic in North Ogden in 1979. The goal was to make intermediate, low-cost healthcare available to areas somewhat distant from the hospital. In addition, the hospital employed specialists. With this groundwork, the hospital was ideally situated when Intermountain decided, in 1994, to develop its own group of clinics and physicians throughout the system. Intermountain Healthcare established the Intermountain Medical Group (originally called the Physician Division), whose sole purpose was to develop and manage these physician practices.

Under the leadership of Medical Director Jerry Gardner, MD, and Operations Director Paul VanWagenen, those initial McKay-Dee practices were incorporated into the Intermountain Medical Group. Today that group includes Layton Clinic (originally Fairfield), Herefordshire Clinic, North Ogden Clinic, South Ogden Clinic, Syracuse Clinic, and a host of practices

This second-generation Intermountain North Ogden Medical Clinic, 2400 N. Washington Boulevard, is on the site of the original facility. The McKay-Dee Medical Clinic opened September 25, 1979. It was the first outreach clinic conceived by Administrator Ken Johnson.

on the hospital campus. Through the years, the Medical Group has continued to meet the needs of its growing population by expanding existing clinics and opening new ones as needed.

HOSPITALISTS

From the opening of the new hospital in 2002, Intermountain McKay-Dee and the Intermountain Medical Group embraced the emergence of the hospitalist, an internal medicine specialist who provides general medical care for hospitalized patients ages 18 and older. In 2010, 11 hospitalists carry the bulk of the hospital's patient load.

"It's hard for physicians in private practice to see all of their office patients, plus spend mornings or afternoons doing rounds here at the hospital," says Intermountain McKay-Dee Chief Medical Officer Dr. Richard Arbogast. But a hospitalist is always available, 24/7. The use of McKay-Dee hospitalists is purely voluntary, but almost 100 physicians in Weber and Davis counties have made the arrangement. Because of medicine's increasing complexity, on-site hospitalists are in the best position to provide treatment, update a patient's family about their loved one's condition, address specific concerns, and answer questions.

NURSING IN OGDEN MAKES ITS MARK

"Annie's vision of the future was absolutely incredible – near prophetic! She understood that, in order to have wonderful healthcare in the community, there needed to be qualified staff, particularly nursing staff that would have the skill and caring to address the needs of the growing population," says Tim Pehrson, CEO of Intermountain McKay-Dee Hospital Center. "Many things have changed over these last 100 years, but the one thing that hasn't is the need for strong, qualified nurses to take care of our patients. Annie's vision of embedding a nurse training program into the Dee Hospital led to a culture of nurse education that continues today in our wonderful relationship with Weber State University's nursing program and the local applied technology colleges."

ESTABLISHING THE THOMAS D. DEE MEMORIAL HOSPITAL SCHOOL OF NURSING

The Thomas D. Dee Memorial Hospital School of Nursing was established along with the new hospital facility in 1910. It was the first formal nursing school in Utah. Nurses assisted with surgeries, provided pain relief and comfort, and dispensed pharmaceuticals such as morphine.

Nursing students provided a major part of nursing care of the hospital, doing virtually all of their practical, clinical training on the job with the patients while under the supervision of head nurses. Student nurses were also expected to perform special private-duty care in the hospital and in homes as part of their training and with no compensation.

The labor of student nurses was so important to daily hospital operations that, for the first few years, classes were held only after the workday. Nursing students worked 12-hour shifts — with a two-hour break, if it wasn't too busy — and began classes at 7 p.m. in the hospital basement with physicians as instructors. In 1912, new caps, pins, and uniforms — which were white with narrow blue stripes and featured stiff white collars and white bibbed aprons over ankle-length skirts worn with black shoes — were designed for Dee nurses and remained in use until 1917.

The first graduation exercises, in 1913, were held for eight students in the auditorium of Weber College. To celebrate the achievement, specially designed diplomas were presented by Annie Taylor Dee and Annie J. Hall, who had taken over the nursing school in 1912. They also presented newly styled graduation pins modeled after a Roman coin. Nurses also

Nurses in 1910 were instructed by a lecturing staff of physicians and professionals who covered a thorough curriculum of coursework, quite comprehensive for medical practice as it was known a hundred years ago. Several of these physician and registered nurse instructors continued lecturing for many years.

Physician Instructors	Class Subjects Taught
Dr. Robert S. Joyce	*First Aid & Surgery*
Dr. Ezra Rich	*Gynecology*
Dr. LeRoy Pugmire	*Eye, Ear, Nose & Throat*
Dr. Paul Ingebretsen	*Materia Medica*
Dr. McCune	*Solutions*
Dr. E.I. Rich	*Obstetrics*
Dr. Eugene Smith	*Pediatrics*
Dr. A.A. Robinson	*Neurology*
Dr. Joseph Morrell	*Anatomy, Physiology & Contagious Diseases*
Dr. Walter Whalen	*Bacteriology*
Dr. R.E. Worrell	*Venereal Disease*
Miss Annie J. Hall	*Practical Points in Nursing & Nursing Ethics*
Dr. O.S. Osgood	*Surgery*
Dr. E.P. Mills	*Contagious Diseases*
Miss Martiner	*Dietetics*
Miss Neilson	*Swedish Massage*

recited the Florence Nightingale Pledge.

LDS Church Apostle, David O. McKay, in his address to nursing graduates, emphasized the qualities necessary for the successful nurse, including self-sacrifice and hard work. He declared, "The community owes a debt of gratitude to Mrs. Dee and her children for the building of the hospital which makes possible the giving of better attention to the afflicted."

Hall is credited with expanding the 2 1/2-year nursing school program to a three-year program in 1913 after increasing curriculum standards. The students' half-day off each week might have been spent studying. The expanded nursing program required theory and practical experience in surgery, medicine, dietetics, first aid, ear, nose and throat, venereal and other contagious disease, gynecology, neurology, physiology, bacteriology, nursing ethics, and Swedish massage.

Because there was no obstetrical division at that time, Annie Hall, through the generous support of Annie Taylor Dee, opened an obstetrical division at the Dee. Annie Taylor Dee encouraged expectant mothers to become hospital-minded by paying the hospital fee of $25 for a 14-day stay. Doctors and head nurses trained student nurses in how to take over the duties home midwives had given in the past and to provide postpartum hospital care to mothers and their newborns.

In 1915, Stella Sainsbury, a graduate of the LDS Hospital School of Nursing, was appointed superintendent of nurses at the Dee.

Classes and living quarters for nurses remained in the hospital basement until the student body grew so much that Maude Dee Porter acquired some nearby houses to serve as living quarters while the Nursing Home was being built adjacent to the hospital.

THE FLORENCE NIGHTINGALE PLEDGE

I solemnly pledge myself before God and in the presence of this assembly to pass my life in purity and to practice my profession faithfully. I will abstain from whatever is deleterious and mischievous, and will not take or knowingly administer any harmful drug. I will do all in my power to elevate the standard of my profession and will hold in confidence all personal matters committed to my keeping, and all family affairs coming to my knowledge in the practice of my calling. With loyalty will I endeavor to aid the physician in his work and devote myself to the welfare of those committed to my care.

— pledge taken by Dee Nursing School graduates

This dorm room for two student nurses to live, work, and study exemplifies the spare charm of wooden furniture, chintz curtains and bedspreads, no phone or radio, but a clock to wake them early and remind them of their 10 p.m. curfew – unless they were assisting on a night shift.

On August 24, 1917, the Thomas D. Dee Memorial School of Nursing and the Dee Memorial Hospital Nursing Home were dedicated. The nursing home dormitory was beautifully furnished with a piano, phonograph, and recordings of popular Hawaiian music. Students, who could not be married, were housed two women to a room for their three years of training. Student rooms featured built-in dressing tables with glass tops over flowered chintz. Each nurse had her own closet and drawer space, and slept in a twin bed. Student nurses had a 10 p.m. curfew, which was enforced by a house mother. Once a month, the nursing students could stay out until midnight.

Night duty in the hospital was handled by student nurses — one to each of the four floors. Sometimes, a student nurse would help the nurse with the lightest patient load cook the midnight meal for nurses and student nurses.

Classes were held in a larger room in the basement that doubled as a rec room. X-ray technique and anesthesia instruction were added as required classes in 1918 and 1919.

The first graduates of the Thomas D. Dee Memorial Hospital School of Nursing in 1913 were:

Anna Hansen *of Ogden*

Ethel Edwards *of Ogden*

Marie Rasmussen *of Ogden*

Lucille Dunbar VanDyke *of San Francisco, Calif.*

Jean Sharp of *Evanston, Wyo.*

Leota Embling Hooper *of Ogden*

Francis Burrell Anderson *of Davis City, Iowa*

Ruth Harbison Freed *of Ogden*

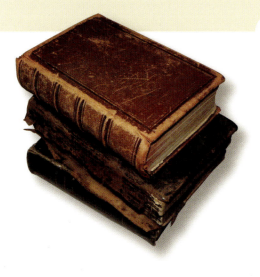

Top: In 1917, the Thomas D. Dee Memorial School of Nursing and the Dee Memorial Hospital Nursing Home were dedicated. Among dignitaries photographed on the outside steps are LDS Church President Joseph F. Smith and hospital nurses and nursing school founder Annie Taylor Dee, wearing the light-colored hat.

Bottom: The nurses in training in 1917 wore newly designed ankle-length white uniform dresses with starched collars, cuffs, and white bibbed aprons. Their hose and shoes were black. Eight to a dozen students per class lived in the new dormitory, during their three-year training commitment.

Supervisors and student nurses pose for a portrait on November 10, 1919, outside the Dee. Two of the nursing school instructors are seen in front: Dr. H.G. Adams and Dr. J.R. Morrell, the latter of whom taught anatomy and physiology and contagious diseases.

WAR AND THE INFLUENZA PANDEMIC OF 1917–19

Nearly concurrent with the opening of the Dee School of Nursing and the Nursing Home east of the hospital in 1917, the United States entered World War I. Superintendent of Nurses Stella Sainsbury enlisted, and Stella Peterson, a fellow graduate of the LDS Hospital School of Nursing, replaced her. Because nurses were so badly needed to help with the wounded, five nursing graduates from the class of 1918 volunteered and were sent overseas as soon as it was learned they had been schooled in administering anesthesia.

The Influenza Pandemic of 1917-1919 also put a great strain on the hospital, nursing staff and the school. The pandemic killed more people than the losses of World War I. Studies suggest at least 30 million people — and perhaps as many as 100 million — died worldwide. Just as the war was winding down, a fifth of the world's population was infected. As a result, the average life span in the United States was reduced by 10 years.

Known as "Spanish Flu," the epidemic forced the construction of temporary frame quarters, the Annex, north of the Dee. The nurses had direct contact with virally infected patients years before the medical community knew about communicable viral diseases, disposable gloves, immunization, and antiviral medications. The long hours put in by these students, and the resulting stress and fatigue they and their supervising nurses experienced, put them at great risk for contracting the life-threatening infection. Very few nurses escaped the flu. Each student remained off duty only long enough to recover from the initial symptoms. Two Dee student nurses were listed among the fatalities.

The second and third floors, delivery room, patient rooms and ward, and even hallways, were filled with flu patients.

In their starched caps and tailored white uniforms of a bygone era, Dee Hospital nursing graduates of 1930 pose outside of the Dee Hospital at 24th Street and Harrison Boulevard. Nursing graduates had to be 21 years old to be licensed to work in Utah. Many had to wait for a birthday to take a job.

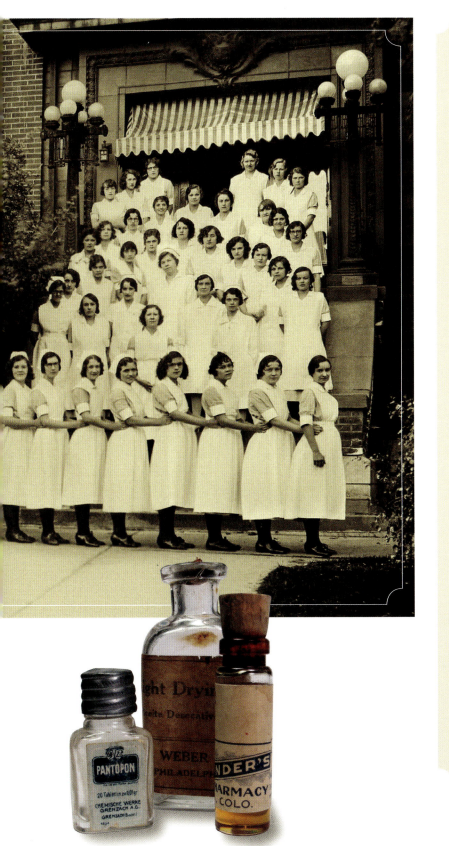

Nurses and student nurses made their own cotton balls, sharpened needles and knives for the operating room, learned to sterilize thermometers, and paid for broken ones. They taped (paper) sacks (for used tissues, etc.) to beds, made up patient beds with fresh linens, and passed out medications. Nurses also gave bed baths and managed bedpans, which were carried down the halls for disposal.

Surgical nurses sharpened needles, mended, washed and powdered gloves and restored the operating room to order after surgeries were finished. Sterilizing and "doing up the packets" for each type of operation were all part of the nurses' duties. Needles had to be threaded with black silk thread or cotton, depending upon where in the body the surgery was to take place. A retired nurse recalls, "Needles didn't come threaded like they do now, and there was no cauterizing a bleeding vessel. We had to tie them off by hand."

Sometimes, entire families were hospitalized. The basement served as a morgue and was constantly filled. The fourth floor and operating rooms were quarantined from the rest of the hospital during the epidemic, and only emergency surgery was performed. The Annex remained in use as an isolation unit until 1920.

After the war, nurses worked from 7 a.m. to 6 p.m., with two hours' worth of classes tucked into their day. Throughout the Roaring '20s and early '30s, night-shift nurses reported to work at 6 p.m.

While a graduate nurse supervised, students ran the operating room and delivery room, and administered emergency anesthetics. They ran the business office, admitting and releasing patients — even totaling their bills. They operated the switchboard, staffed the information desk, and cooked and served the midnight meal for the other employees. One student was often responsible for 30 to 35 very ill patients.

In 1925, students were given the option of wearing a cape with the name of the nursing school on the collar, but not all students could afford one.

In 1926, a new department called Public Health, or "clinic," was added to the hospital to provide additional training for nurses. No other nursing school in Utah had such a department, which usually had three or four nurses in training at a time. They worked in city-financed venereal disease clinics and well-baby clinics. When the Ogden City/Weber County Health District was formed in 1936, the Dee's 10-year-old Public Health Department was closed.

A Retired Nurse Remembers

In 1931, the capping ceremony was introduced for student nurses, and in 1932, the nursing school affiliated with Weber College. Nursing graduates had to be 21 years old to be

Nurses didn't listen to heart or lung sounds,
nor use gloves very often except in surgery.

•

Nurses were required to stand up respectfully when a doctor came
into the room. Instilled in them during their training were basic nursing skills,
obedience to doctors' orders, and professionalism.

•

Nurses worked a 12-hour day with one-half day per week off
when the patient load permitted.

licensed to work in Utah. Many who were younger had to wait to take a job. The strict lifestyle and training standards continued for another generation.

Josephine Manning, a retired nurse in her 80s who began training in 1940, recalls, "At graduation, we had caps, gowns, and dark blue capes with beautiful red lining. By then, the Dee Hospital Nursing School uniforms were white shirtwaist-type dresses with short sleeves, white belts, no bibs, and no aprons. We wore white nylons and white shoes instead of black, no high-heels, and no open-toes. That year, a black ribbon on the cap became an honor bestowed only upon graduation. Rules were strict. We would be called into the office if our shoelaces weren't clean or we didn't wear our belts."

She remembers: "Nursing school tuition was $100 for the whole three years, and back in 1940, that was a lot of money. We were given room and board and worked eight-hour shifts or longer. After a while, we did get a little money — $5 a month, which was very helpful. We students slept and literally lived at the hospital because we still could not be married and had to live in the dorm. A 'big sister' — a junior or senior nurse — looked after each student," she said.

"Senior nurses really had us little probies (first-year students) scared," Manning says. "After six months, we received our plain white caps and worked on the floor eight hours a day, five days a week, and had classes besides. Caps had one stripe when we started. Our second year, we received a second stripe, and our third year, our third stripe was awarded in a capping exercise at graduation."

Manning recalls concluding her studies in 1944. "After graduation, we could heal the sick and get paid for it. We could even get married and start our families. Many of us returned to nursing after our families were raised."

NURSING THROUGH WORLD WAR II

The Japanese attack on Pearl Harbor on December 7, 1941, changed nursing dramatically. When war was declared by the United States, many Dee Hospital doctors and nurses, including Dee Nursing School physician instructors, responded to the armed services' call for trained medical personnel. Faced with a shortage of nurses, the U.S. Cadet Nurses Corps, from its creation in 1942 to its dissolution in 1949, recruited by paying a stipend, plus covering students' tuition, uniforms, and books. With the resulting shortage in the Dee Hospital, student nurses were taught procedures more quickly and did more of the work than they would have if there had been no war. They helped in the delivery room and the emergency room. Everyone worked long hours. But, one retired nurse says, "It was an exciting time because we geared up to do our part, were keyed up, and felt united in a common purpose to help in the war effort."

Many nurses who had retired came back to help during the war or took up private-duty nursing, where they could choose their hours. "We were much in demand at $18 for a 12-hour shift," recalls a nurse alumna. "That was a marked improvement over $5 per shift during the Great Depression, or a basket of vegetables from someone's garden."

The Dee Hospital School of Nursing graduating class of 1944 was so small because of the war and the Great Depression that graduation exercises were held with the class of 1945 and still totaled fewer than 10 graduates.

The close friendships that grew between student nurses living and working together at the Dee Hospital, particularly during the war years, lasted for their lifetimes. The Thomas D. Dee Memorial Hospital School of Nursing Alumni Association, formed in 1913, remains active to this day with an impressive 97-year history.

Soldiering Through the Polio Epidemic

The *Ogden Standard-Examiner* newspaper of January 1938 stated that, "Common communicable diseases in Ogden are chicken pox, scarlet fever, influenza, mumps, whooping cough, and Infantile Paralysis (polio). Polio was contracted by President Franklin Delano Roosevelt, and prompted him to initiate his Warm Springs Foundation for treatment of the disease, particularly for children so afflicted."

Those early years of Infantile Paralysis were precursors of what came to be known in Ogden and throughout the country as the polio epidemic. During that epidemic, there was a shortage of nurses. A member of the Dee Nurses Alumni recalls, "As nursing students, we had 'the privilege' of signing up with the American Red Cross to be volunteers, should anything tragic happen. With the polio epidemic in the '40s and '50s, we were called to work in the only polio wards in Ogden, which were at St. Benedict's Hospital.

"There were three iron lungs in a huge room. Nurses lived in that room for their eight-hour shifts with those three patients. We'd go from one to the next, clearing their lungs, trying to help them breathe."

1944 Lucin Train Wreck

On New Year's Eve, 1944, there was a train wreck on the Lucin Cut-off, a shortcut across Great Salt Lake. One train ran into the end of another. It was one of the nation's worst train disasters; 48 were killed and 79 were injured. Many were servicemen. It was more expedient to put some of the injured men on a train to Ogden than on a train to San Francisco, but still some didn't make it. Nurse Josephine Manning recalls, "The hospital had a makeshift morgue on the first floor in the office area until the Army could come and collect the bodies of those who perished. It brought the war home to us at the Dee Hospital in a vivid and heartbreaking way."

The case for (train company) negligence was taken all the way to the U. S. Supreme Court. Medical examiners determined the engineer had died of a heart attack before the accident. "A dead man was at the throttle at the time of the wreck," according to a quote in a newspaper article.

In 1944, nurses and doctors first administered the antibiotic penicillin at the Dee Hospital. Many more patients who were critically ill with infections resulting from disease or injury were saved than had ever been possible. Antibiotics seemed to make miracles happen.

Carol Godfrey and Sally Whitehead, both nurses at Intermountain McKay-Dee with more than 40 years of experience, completed their clinical internships at the Dee Hospital.

"Back then," Godfrey recalls, "the only air conditioning in the whole building was in the six-bed Coronary Care unit. We used to open windows to make patients more comfortable."

Whitehead remembers, "McKay Hospital, previous to the current Intermountain McKay-Dee Hospital Center, had air conditioning throughout and monitors for most units. Opening windows is not allowed now."

NURSING INSTRUCTION BECOMES MORE DEMANDING

A more comprehensive coursework program was in place by the 1940s. The Nursing Arts Laboratory included advancements made in teaching content and methods from 1917 to 1930. Many instructors participated in the arts-lab approach to "modern" teaching methods. As enrollment increased over the succeeding years, nursing classes were held during the day and were offered by different instructors at the same hour, as subjects and techniques were taught separately for first-year, second-year, and third-year students.

Anatomy, Anesthetics, Charting, Contagious Diseases, Dietetics, Essentials of Medicine, First Aid with an emphasis on wound care and bandaging, Hydrotherapy, Massage, Nervous Disorders, Nursing Ethics, Obstetrics, and Operating Techniques were presented in lectures, with all student nurses given hands-on supervised experience with hospital patients. Students learned Draping Techniques, which included preparing patients for surgery, then assisting the surgeon. Cold Baths and Packs, Arrangement of Pillows for Comfort, Bed Baths, Postoperative Care, and Postmortem Care were also standard training.

In 1942, the Dee Nursing School became affiliated with the University of Utah in Salt Lake City, so third-year students could receive instruction in tuberculosis and psychiatric nursing. The five-year program was later discontinued when the University of Utah changed to a four-year program.

In the 1950s, the Nursing Arts Lab in the Dee Nursing School included classwork in Inhalers and Steam Techniques to ease breathing, Oxygen Therapies, and Sterile Glove and Gown procedures. A new offering was the Principles of Psychiatry class

Weber State University School of Nursing

Weber State College School of Nursing, established in 1955, was the first academic nursing school in the nation. Now Weber State University has one of the best training programs for nurses, attracting applicants from across the United States. Nursing students do their clinical training at the Intermountain McKay-Dee Hospital Center. In 2009, 381 students graduated from the Weber State University School of Nursing.

A few students get their nursing degrees before going to medical school. "Nursing is no longer just something students, particularly women, do to 'have something to fall back on' when they marry and have families," says Chief Nurse Bonnie Jacklin. "Our nurse employees are proud men and women professionals with a significant voice for program improvements here at the Intermountain McKay-Dee Hospital Center. Offering practical experience and inspiration to young Weber State University nursing students is our privilege."

taught by Dr. William H. Megordon and Mrs. Edna Seidner. The class lectures included what was known at the time as manifestations of psychoses for dementia and diseases such as venereal ailments and meningitis that caused abnormal behaviors in patients.

Nursing school instruction continued to evolve at the Dee to meet growing academic and financial expectations by aligning coursework with Weber College in Ogden. However, in 1955, the Dee School of Nursing and Weber College participated in a national study involving six other community colleges and their hospital affiliates. It found that the nursing field required more medical and scientific knowledge than the nursing schools were providing.

That same year, the Dee School of Nursing was phased out and Weber College took over all classes. Superior classroom training at the college followed the high standards that had been set at the Dee Nursing School, and practical work with medical professionals and patients continued at the Dee. The program met expanding needs and capabilities at both

institutions to handle increasing numbers of students requiring hands-on experience.

Meanwhile, the Dee School of Nursing graduated the class of 1955 and presented its last 19 students with diplomas. A total of 720 students were graduated during the Dee School of Nursing's 45 years. The cooperative nature of textbook instruction at what has since become Weber State University and the practical clinical experience at what is now Intermountain McKay-Dee Hospital Center continues today. Once nurses are on the job at McKay-Dee, they are encouraged to participate in professional organizations and to attend regional and national seminars so they can stay up on the latest technology and treatment options. Many return with stories of how remarkably well known throughout the nation McKay-Dee Hospital is for its consistently high-quality healthcare and nursing opportunities.

Breaking Down Barriers

By the 1980s, more men were training to be nurses. "For some, nursing is a stepping stone to becoming a physician's assistant or a nurse anesthetist or a nurse practitioner. The phenomenal growth in technical aspects of modern nursing care appeals to men," Chief Nurse Bonnie Jacklin said in a 1980 hospital employee newsletter.

At that time, McKay-Dee already had plenty of male nurses and a number in the pipeline: 31 on staff and 11 as students. Men, however, faced special challenges in nursing. Terry Baxter, an Emergency Room staff nurse in 1980, said in an employee newsletter that year, "People always think you're a doctor and expect you to do the doctor's job. The other thing that irks me is being labeled a 'male nurse.' We know we're males and, hopefully, so does everyone else around us. Why not just call us nurses?"

He also said women aren't the only ones who can give tender, loving care. "I've had patients tell me that men are more gentle when it comes to scrubbing wounds. You have to be a caring person to even want to be a nurse in the first place."

Jacklin said McKay-Dee is also special because of its long-tenured nurses. "There's a generational tradition here for many of us who have nurses in our families. You have from a 21-year-old to a 60-year-old nurse on the same unit — what an opportunity for the young ones to learn."

"One thing all nurses learn to do is empathize with patients," Jacklin said.

"Nurses really care for you. It's not so much the tasks they perform as the connection, the touch, the listening, and the comfort. We are committed to helping patients feel safe, welcome, and at ease. Our Healing Connections program trains nurses to suspend judgment about a patient and express caring. There is a clinical touch, like taking blood pressure, then there is the touch of sincere caring that relieves anxiety, builds trust, and begins healing."

Jacklin is proud of how the program makes nurses stop and think. She adds, "The Healing Connections program has helped nurses better connect with their patients. It's what good nursing is all about."

Nursing Services in the Women and Newborns Department

McKay-Dee has also become respected for progress in its Women and Newborns Department. The hospital's Intensive Care Nursery was initially funded by a $10,000 gift from Mrs. Edith Budge as a living memorial to her husband, Dr. W.C. Budge, who delivered hundreds of babies at the Thomas D. Dee Memorial Hospital during his distinguished medical career.

In 1972, it was reported that McKay-Dee led the Intermountain area in the development of infant-care services. From 1970 through 1971, the hospital's deaths per thousand live births declined to 10.39, considerably below the national rate in 1970 of 14.9 deaths per thousand births.

The hospital continued improving in this area over the years, and a May 1992 employee newsletter reports that more than 40,000 infants in the U.S. died because of low birthweight, but McKay-Dee's Newborn Intensive Care Unit ranked second in a study of 36 major U.S. hospitals for success with low-birthweight babies. The hospital has Northern Utah's largest Perinatal Service specializing in diagnosing and treating high-risk pregnancies. Physicians from Northern Utah, Southern Idaho and Western Wyoming refer complicated pregnancies to McKay-Dee because of its success.

A big factor in that success, the newsletter reports, is McKay-Dee's team of specialists: doctors board certified in O.B. Anesthesia and working in the Labor & Delivery unit 24 hours a day; doctors who specialize in high-risk pregnancies and infants; nursing staff certified in neonatal life support; and medical residents in Labor & Delivery able to assist when and where needed.

Because time is crucial in an emergency, McKay-Dee could meet or beat the best in the country in performing emergency cesarean sections — six minutes or less to save a baby in distress when the national standard is 30 minutes, according to a May 1992 employee newsletter.

Today at McKay-Dee, expectant mothers can prepare — body, mind, and spirit — for having a baby through a variety of childbirth education classes.

Registering for Childbirth Preparation, Lamaze, or Hypnobirthing — for $45, $55, and $140, respectively — means being able to take classes in Breastfeeding, Baby Care, or Infant Massage for free. The hospital also offers a free Young Moms class that covers what to expect during pregnancy, labor and delivery, and when the infant comes home. Also available are prenatal fitness classes to help prepare the body for the rigors of delivery, as well as classes for children so they can prepare for being a big brother or sister.

Left: When plans for the new McKay Hospital were on the drawing boards, intensive care for infants was only a dream in the minds of a few farsighted health professionals. It became a reality at the new facility that opened in 1969.

Inset: On October 24, 1984, Francie Garrett, RN, helps get new mother Beverly Murray to her car using one of McKay-Dee Hospital's double umbrellas that protect the mother and her newborn. These new umbrellas were distributed to all nursing floors just in time for winter.

Facing: Roberta Dixon, RN, assists a mother with her newborn infant.

In the spring of 1975, Mrs. Sue Henderson, a Certified Nurse-Midwife (the only one in Ogden at the time), served as McKay-Dee clinical director for the labor, delivery, nursery, and postpartum areas. She saw her role as "developing a continuum of care" and advocated breaking down walls to achieve complete cooperation and coordination between the hospital's maternity and childcare areas.

McKay-Dee Home Health Services

Above: Registered Nurse Hilma Carver exits her white Rambler on a Home Care visit to a patient in 1970. Begun in 1963 with an initial grant from the Annie Taylor Dee Foundation, McKay-Dee Home Health Services ran Utah's first and, for many years, only hospital-based home healthcare program. In 1970, charges were $8 an hour for skilled nursing or therapeutic care. Nurse aides charged $4 per hour. Some Home Care nurses reported driving as far as 40 miles a day in 1970. Note the McKay-Dee emblem "dedication, empathy, excellence" on the car door.

Facing, inset: Helping hands and the "little black bag" of the McKay-Dee Home Health Services nurses became more evident during the 1970s with a reported monthly patient average of 49.25. The number of treatments for these patients averaged 678.5 visits a month.

Above: McKay-Dee Home Health Services took on even greater emphasis at McKay-Dee during the 1980s as a large portion of the population entered their senior years. The administration and medical staff of the McKay-Dee stated its redefined purpose "to lead out in the delivery of high-quality hospital care to an ever-increasing segment of the population."

The Telecare Program for the aged and disabled was operated by volunteers who provided comforting telephone contact with confined persons once every 24 hours. Hospital nurses responded as necessary.

Healing at Home

After World War II, Dee Nursing School and Weber College nursing graduates were in high demand for their superior training and professional standards. Many nurses followed their husbands throughout the nation, wherever work could be found. They sometimes left nursing to raise their families and returned to become recertified when their children were grown, often working into their senior years.

They provided nursing and social services for the homebound elderly, patients in nursing homes, at air bases, on the railroads, at Yellowstone's veterans hospital, and in coal-mining communities. Many credited their successful nursing careers to their excellent preparation through rigorous instruction. Quite a few graduates from the Ogden area volunteered in their communities after their "formal" retirement.

Many began working in McKay-Dee's official Home Care program, which was created in 1963. It was a revolutionary idea for a hospital-based agency at that time. The federal government didn't begin such a program in Utah until 1970, and most home health agencies weren't started until the early 1980s. As hospital costs rose, insurance companies began limiting the length of patient stays, requiring more care in the home. Medicare and Medicaid also played roles in the increasing need for home healthcare.

Some Home Care nurses helped seniors make their homes safe and convenient. Some helped parents learn how to take over care of their babies going home after an extended stay in the Newborn Intensive Care Unit. Some helped paraplegics avoid bedsores and provided physical therapy.

Home aides were trained in CPR and rendering assistance where needed, be it bathing, shopping, cooking, cleaning — anything to make life easier for homebound patients and to help them maintain their quality of life.

Home Care nurses also addressed the emotional aspects many families face with seniors approaching the end of their life.

In a 1991 employee newsletter, Carolyn Tometich, the supervisor of the Ogden Home Care office, said, "It's hard to be realistic about your loved ones dying. They are home with the family in a happy, familiar environment, but being hooked to a machine doesn't make them 21 again and well."

At the very least, she said, Home Care nurses tried to make the end as peaceful as possible for the patient and the family, and to prepare them for what was coming.

"We become part of the family for a portion of time," Noreen Rylander, a pediatric nurse in the hospital's Home Care program, said in the employee newsletter. "You have to let the human side of yourself come out and bond in some way with the patient and family. If you don't, they won't let you back in the house. They have to feel that they can ask you anything."

Now, home healthcare is a separate program run by Intermountain Healthcare rather than by individual hospitals.

The Art of Healing: A Century of Nursing Care

Educating nurses to make a healing difference was a vital component of Annie Taylor Dee's vision for hospital care. Her plan for onsite nurses' training developed in conjunction with the construction of Thomas D. Dee Memorial Hospital. In 1910, she understood well the need for local medical training in the best methods of her day.

A hundred years ago, she made career options possible for Ogden-area women. In the words of one retired nurse, "Annie started something wonderful, a real healing gift to the community, and a dignified way to earn a living for career nurses."

Annie's vision included preparing registered nurses to care for ensuing generations of area residents. The hospital's partnership with Weber State University's nursing program continues to be a foundation of McKay-Dee's healthcare efforts in the community.

In 2010, most of McKay-Dee's nurses are graduates of

Weber State University's School of Nursing in the Allied Health Department who gained practical student experience at McKay-Dee. Some of today's nurses started as Candy Striper teen volunteers at the original Dee. McKay-Dee's more than 900 full- and part-time nurses range in age from their 20s to their 60s, with 43 being the average age of a McKay-Dee nurse.

All of the hospital's nurses — despite their backgrounds and beginnings — have common goals: to keep a patient alive, to alleviate suffering, and to promote recovery.

"They have more interactions with patients than anyone else," says Chief Nurse Bonnie Jacklin. "They often spend more time with each other and their patients than they do with their own families."

Today's nurse is as likely to be a man as a woman, and all appear at the bedside in colorful, practical scrubs. All try to keep a cheerful attitude to comfort and relax patients who are in a stressful situation and out of their element.

Nursing specialties run the gamut from critical care to the Operating Room, the Emergency Department, palliative care for easing pain and other debilitating symptoms, newborn and premature babies, and women's and children's care, to name a few. Today's nurses care for recovering surgical patients or those being treated for an infectious illness with shorter stays than in the past.

Increasing regulation, documenting, tracking, and following up with patients require new skills. Nurses have become masters of computer data collection and archiving for each patient. They have also become educators who must teach patients and family caregivers how to continue treatment regimens and healing at home.

Nurse Carol Godfrey says, "Disclosure used to be up to the doctors at the original Dee Hospital, but these days, patients have the right and need to know everything possible about their medical conditions, treatments, and expectations for recovery."

Nurse Sally Whitehead agrees, saying, "As nurses, we are advocates of patient education. We inform patients and prepare them to take an active role in their recovery and ongoing medical needs after they leave the hospital."

Jacklin speaks of Annie Taylor Dee with reverence. "She began something that has snowballed. Annie's vision a hundred years ago, has had a direct impact on my life as a nurse at the McKay-Dee Hospital."

To be professionally trained in medical treatment is vital in hospital care, but to be a wise and compassionate caregiver, able to treat emotional as well as medical needs, is what it takes to be a really good nurse. A nurse is more than a dispenser of medicines, an assessor of vital signs, a provider of treatment – a nurse is a nurturer, a giver of comfort and hope as well as clinical expertise in support of physicians. Patients want to be "nursed" back to health when they come to McKay-Dee Hospital Center. There is an art to being a professional nurse who treats and calms a patient in support of the healing process.

THE PEOPLE BEHIND *the* SCENES

BACK IN 1905, WHEN HER HUSBAND DIED, ANNIE TAYLOR DEE CHOSE TO MEMORIALIZE HIM BY GIVING BACK TO HER COMMUNITY. SHE REALIZED THE FAST-GROWING OGDEN COMMUNITY WAS IN DIRE NEED OF A HOSPITAL TO PROVIDE ACUTE CARE FOR THOSE WITH SERIOUS ILLNESSES AND INJURIES. ANNIE, WHO HAD BEEN ACTIVE IN THE LEADERSHIP OF THE LDS CHURCH'S RELIEF SOCIETY, WAS FAMILIAR WITH THE IMPORTANCE OF COMMUNITY SERVICE AND THE DRIVE NEEDED TO FULFILL LARGE AMBITIONS.

She saw how her family — being blessed with financial security — could contribute to building a long-lasting asset for the community.

Her family funds established the hospital and kept it running until 1915, when the family gave the facility to the LDS Church. Even though the hospital was no longer under her direct supervision, Annie and her family continued to financially support it and its endeavors. Today, her descendants still contribute to the hospital and the well-being of the community, keeping alive Annie's legacy and dedication to the health of the area's residents. She would be proud to know their generosity — a hundred years later — still sustains the hospital and honors her husband, Thomas Duncombe Dee.

The original Dee was built before antibiotics, blood-type matching, and transfusion technology, when oxygen therapy was delivered by placing tents over patients' beds and premature babies rarely survived. Progress came one piece of equipment,

one new development, at a time, each year building on the last.

But buildings serve little purpose without people. Through the last hundred years, the generosity of Annie and her descendants have been essential to the progress of the hospital and quality of medical care.

The Dee family tree is quite extensive, as is its members' giving and support. Dee family members are leaders in philanthropy, as demonstrated by their giving, both personally and through their family foundations. Lawrence T. Dee, Annie's son along with his wife, Janet, gave their financial support, according to historical documents. In 1971, the couple started the Lawrence T. and Janet T. Dee Foundation with the goal of enhancing quality of life in the community.

Thomas D. Dee II, Lawrence's son and at that time a hospital board member, and his first wife, Elizabeth, continued the family's tradition of giving by supporting numerous hospital projects. Before his death, he and his wife, Janice, paid tribute to his grandmother by naming Intermountain McKay-Dee Hospital's new guest home after Annie Taylor Dee. That home, which opened on the McKay-Dee complex during the hospital's centennial anniversary, provides hotel-like accommodations as well as a place of comfort and peace for family members of critically ill or injured hospital patients who are far from home.

The Edith Dee Green Foundation, in memory of one of Annie's daughters, and the Mary Elizabeth Dee Shaw Foundation, in memory of another, financially supported the building of McKay-Dee Hospital and its Stewart Rehabilitation Center. A third daughter, Margaret Dee Higginbotham, and granddaughters Margaret Dee Higginbotham Madsen and Dorothy Higginbotham Stevenson contributed to the hospital's causes. The Stewart Education Foundation was organized in memory of Annie's granddaughter Elizabeth Shaw Stewart. Annie's grandsons, Harold and Dee Wade Mack, and their wives, Shirley and Melva, respectively, contributed to the Edith Dee Green Education Center and the remodeling of the Intensive Care Unit and the Critical Care Unit/Cardiac Unit at McKay-Dee Hospital. Granddaughter-in-law Melva Bronson Mack has given financial support, and now, Annie's great-grandchildren have taken up her cause.

Former foundation board member Barbara Wheat and her husband, Kelly, as well as Janet Mack Palmer and her brother Glen Mack, support the hospital's endeavors. Dee Ann Nye and her husband, Jay, began the annual tradition of the Jaynie Nye Memorial Concert featuring Emmy Award-winning composer and pianist Kurt Bestor. The dinner/concert event honors the courage of the Nyes' daughter Jaynie, who died of cancer in 1980 at age 15, and benefits the Val and Ann Browning Cancer Center at McKay-Dee.

Annie's great-grandsons Tim and David and great-great-grandsons Matt and Nate are current trustees of both the Annie Taylor Dee Foundation and the Lawrence T. and Janet T. Dee Foundation. Tim Dee is also a hospital and foundation board member. He and his wife, Candace, have supported the Annie Taylor Dee Guest Home, as well as many other hospital building projects and patient programs over the years.

McKay-Dee Hospital Board member Jodee Hoellein and Jim, her husband and a former foundation board member, along with their daughter Brittnee, created the Hetzl-Hoellein Foundation. As a family, they support the hospital's Heart Services, are presenting sponsors of Breakfast With Santa, which benefits special-needs children, and also contributed to the Annie Taylor Dee Guest Home in memory of Jodee's grandmother and one of Annie's daughters, Rosabella Cora Dee Barker.

The Dee family's legacy of affordable, accessible, and compassionate healthcare also continues today thanks to the countless hospital employees, volunteers, and other financial donors who take to heart the value of wellness in body, mind, and spirit, and pledge to support the continued expansion of facilities and services that improve health and save the lives of thousands of people living in Northern Utah, Southern Idaho, and Western Wyoming.

Intermountain McKay-Dee Hospital wouldn't exist today without the vision and determination of Annie Taylor Dee, her family, and so many others committed to first-rate medical care and compassion.

The not-for-profit hospital can continue its mission over the next hundred years only through the continued support of those following the example of Annie Taylor Dee and her family. Today's area residents and their descendants are sure to keep that spirit alive through their generous contributions of funds, time, talents, services — and compassion.

The Annual Jaynie Nye Memorial Concert

DeeAnn and Jay Nye appear with Kurt Bestor, (at right) who for 11 years has been the featured performer at the annual Jaynie Nye Memorial Concert and dinner event benefiting the Val and Ann Browning Cancer Center. The Nye family hosts the annual event to honor the courage of their daughter Jaynie, who passed away from cancer in 1980 at age 15.

THE VOLUNTEER AUXILIARY

In 1958, Ruby Wheelwright organized the Thomas D. Dee Memorial Hospital Volunteer Auxiliary, which is affiliated with the American Hospital Association. The first annual meeting was held October 22, followed by the first board meeting on the 31st. Those first meetings established the purpose of the organization — to complement and support the objectives of hospital programs and departments.

More than 3,000 volunteers — men and women, young and old — serve patients from Northern Utah, Southern Idaho, and Western Wyoming, and keep McKay-Dee ranked at the top of the Intermountain Healthcare system for volunteer hours and support activities. In 1993, for example, volunteers donated 55,561 hours; the next year, the number of volunteer hours jumped to 59,530.

Dedicated, talented, and service-oriented volunteers run the hospital gift shop and donate its profits. They staff information desks at the hospital's four entrances, helping patients register and find their way around the facility. They receive and deliver flowers, transport patients via wheelchairs, make patients comfortable, and manage the valet desk, where keys to the cars of outpatients and the disabled are safeguarded. Some volunteers serve as foreign-language interpreters, as well as sign-language interpreters for the hearing impaired. Still others help by bringing their pets in to visit patients undergoing sometimes-difficult rehabilitative therapy.

The Volunteer Auxiliary also holds fundraising events, pledging tens of thousands of dollars every year to benefit hospital causes and hospital departments. For example, it has raised funds to purchase hospital beds for the Intensive Care Unit and equipment for the Newborn Intensive Care Unit.

In 1958, charter members of the Thomas D. Dee Memorial Volunteer Auxiliary who served at the Dee and the subsequent McKay Hospital were, *back row, from left:* Norma Patterson, Evelyna Grace, Janet Dee, Ruth Nelson, director Sara Shaw, Mickey Burdett, Ione Toller, Leager Davis. *Front row, from left:* Marion Schmidt, Elizabeth Stewart, Pat Wecker, founder/chairwoman Ruby Wheelwright, Mary Griffin, Myrene Brewer.

Auxiliary volunteers receive the same hospital orientation as full-time employees and provide vital services in 35 hospital areas. As with the hospital's employee professionals, McKay-Dee's educated and trained volunteers focus on continuous improvement of customer service and staff support.

Weber State University pre-med and pre-nursing, radiology technician, and pharmacy students also learn as they serve as volunteers. Their goal is to earn recommendation letters when they complete their credit and procedural-experience commitments. These students are serious about achieving careers in their chosen medical fields and value their hands-on experience with McKay-Dee medical professionals.

Service opportunities vary. Volunteers can assist in transporting patients to the operating room, help in a variety of capacities in the Women's Center, and work in central supply's materials management. If trained to help registered nurses or anesthesia patients, they assist with intravenous and pulse-taking procedures. Some volunteers assist mothers with their choice of birth plans and often schedule tours of the hospital and its facilities for expectant women and mothers with newborns. The kindness and courtesy of volunteers complements the clinical care provided by the medical staff and actively supports the culture of caring at the McKay-Dee Hospital.

Annie Taylor Dee would be pleased to know her inspiring, compassionate spirit lives on in today's volunteers.

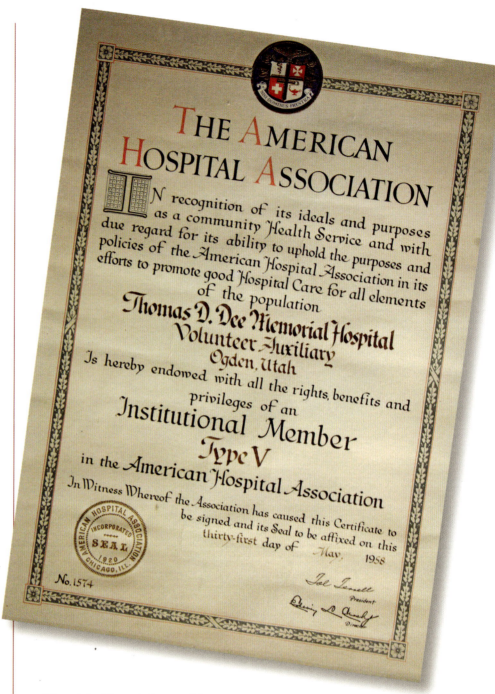

The original framed charter of the Thomas D. Dee Memorial Hospital Volunteer Auxiliary, recognized by the American Hospital Association in May 1958, hangs in the McKay-Dee Hospital Center's Volunteer Offices.

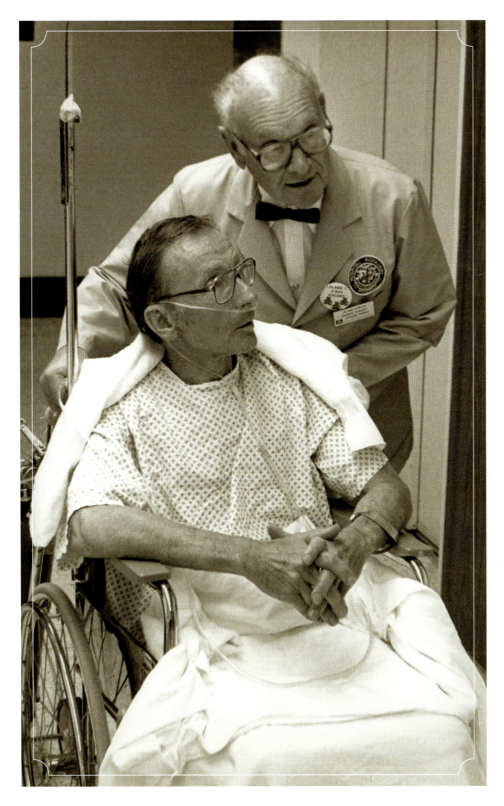

*Volunteers are trained
to fulfill the needs of the
people. They address
challenges with a sense
of commitment, a
sense of urgency, and
personal assistance. It is a
privilege to volunteer in
a professional healthcare
environment, serving those
who trust our care. As
volunteers, we give the gift
of ourselves.*

—*Judy Patterson,
Director of
Volunteer Services*

A volunteer assists a recuperating
patient in his wheelchair at
McKay-Dee Hospital.

Left: The service record is held by Rose Burnett *(left)*, who donated 14,915 hours between 1977 and 1998, and Thelma Laughran, who donated 37,974 hours between 1978 and 2005. Had she been an employee, Thelma would have given more than 25 years of service. Six volunteers have each been active at the hospital for 40 or more years.

Bottom: McKay-Dee Volunteer Auxiliary members Deanna Robinson and Pam Twede assist Karla Lott with her selection at Intermountain McKay-Dee Hospital's gift shop.

THE MCKAY-DEE HOSPITAL FOUNDATION

From the hospital's beginning in 1910, supporting not-for-profit healthcare programs and services for the Ogden community has been central to the Dee legacy. The McKay-Dee Hospital Foundation was formalized as a chartered organization in 1968 to help raise money for the building of what would become McKay-Dee Hospital Center at 3939 Harrison Boulevard.

Since fulfilling that mission, the organization has worked to support patient programs, initiate and sustain community outreach programs, and provide education and preventive services.

Executive Director Cathleen Sparrow says, "The McKay-Dee Hospital Foundation operates through the generosity of community donors who improve and save lives through gifts of equipment that benefit hospital patients and serve the community at large."

Whether accepting financial gifts of a few dollars or those in the millions, Sparrow says, "Every donor dollar is put to use developing and sustaining McKay-Dee programs and services. No gift is insignificant."

The foundation's mission is to be a good steward of donor funds, fulfilling donor desires to make the greatest impact possible by providing exceptional equipment, programs, and education that enhance the hospital's high standard of healthcare and community wellness.

A McKay-Dee Hospital Foundation Wall of Caring in the hospital features the names of individuals, organizations, foundations, schools, and businesses that have contributed $5,000 or more to the well-being of the community. The

The McKay-Dee Hospital Foundation Board of Trustees. The hallmark of the foundation's vision is to be good stewards of donor funds — fulfilling the donors' desire to make the greatest impact with their resources by helping to provide exceptional equipment, programs and education that enhance Intermountain McKay-Dee Hospital's high standard of healthcare and community wellness.

foundation also organizes the Piano Guild, volunteers who play the 9-foot Yamaha Conservatory Grand Piano — one of nine in the United States — in the hospital lobby. The music played on this piano, donated in memory of longtime hospital volunteer and philanthropist Elizabeth Dee Shaw Stewart, helps create a healing environment for patients and their families and helps promote a relaxing atmosphere.

The McKay-Dee Hospital Foundation also sponsors health education forums held quarterly as part of a continuing

Facing: The unique donor-plaque Wall of Caring adjacent to Intermountain McKay-Dee Hospital Center's Main Lobby entrance honors contributions of $5,000 or more since December, 31, 2009.

Above: McKay-Dee Hospital's Women's Council members include, *seated from left*: Marilyn Adams, Lucille Niklason, Dorothy Jones, Diane Russell, G. Linda Hinrichs, Cathleen Sparrow, Shanna Frobin. *Standing from left*: Mary Lou Hammer, Noellee Shaw, Kay Hardy, Rebecca Brockman, Carlene Martindell, Barbara Hoekstra, Geri Hansen, Juanita Watts, Judy Loper, Stacy Durbano, Linda Watson.

education program, plus it holds fundraising events so it can contribute to hospital improvements and advancements.

WOMEN'S COUNCIL

Honoring the desire of Elizabeth Stewart to benefit people with special needs, the Women's Council has worked since 1984 to educate and advocate for community health and wellness in cooperation with the hospital.

The Women's Council plans and promotes educational conferences, screenings, programs, and other opportunities for the benefit of healthcare professionals and the community. The Women's Council works with the McKay-Dee Hospital Foundation to coordinate efforts to address donors' specific interests and the prioritized needs of the hospital. In 2010, there are 30 Women's Council members.

Breakfast With Santa for children with disabilities has been the Women's Council's main fundraising activity

PROVIDING SUPPORT AND INFORMATION

Stroke Support Group

Through camaraderie and sharing, stroke patients learn how to deal with challenges relating to stroke after-effects. Topics on balance, nutrition, driving, and other pertinent information help stroke patients with their daily lives. The Women's Council works with the Stewart Rehabilitation Center in these efforts.

Traumatic Brain Injury Support Group

The Stewart Rehabilitation Center and Women's Council also organize monthly meetings to assist patients with their head injuries and related medical challenges.

Hispanic Labor Friend

Since 2001, Hispanic Labor Friend, with support of the McKay-Dee Foundation and collaborative assistance from Midtown Community Health Center, has sought to assist Spanish-speaking obstetrical patients. Goals include minimizing the language barrier; increasing attention to cultural and social concerns; increasing the patient's ability to make informed choices; and increasing appropriate use of services.

Angel Watch

Designed to help families who learn their baby may have a life-threatening or life-limiting condition, Angel Watch brings together a team of trained professionals to offer support, provide information, and help to design a plan for each family.

since 2000. Through this event, the organization makes a difference in patients' lives by funding hospital programs such as Developmental Screening, the Annie Taylor Dee Guest Home and the Teen Health Lifestyles Program. The Women's Council has also purchased recliners for the NICU and manikin simulators for the pediatric department. Other fundraising efforts provided community health conferences and the award-winning program "A Fine Line."

In Memory of dedicated Women's Council members

We honor these women who were dedicated to the mission of the Women's Council:

Thera Johnson, 1985,
First Chairwoman of the Women's Board
Elizabeth Stewart, 1996
Grand Patron and Honorary Member
Mildred "Mid" Wilson, 1997
Colleen Shreeve, 2002
Jean Wolfert, 2006
Florence Shreeve, 2007
Betty Nowak, Ph.D., 2007
Charter Member, Past Chairwoman
Zada Haws, 2007
Charter Member, Past Chairwoman

Above: The executive team for McKay-Dee Hospital Foundation's Powell Medical Education Open Golf Tournament pose at the fund-raising event. *Front row, from left:* Kassi Bybee, Noellee Shaw, Cathleen Sparrow, Judy Mecham-Swaner, Mary Barker. *Back:* Rex Child.

Top: Each Christmas, the Women's Council holds a Breakfast With Santa for about 75 special-needs youths and their families.

Left: The McKay-Dee Hospital Foundation hosted a '50s stroke support party with "Elvis." *Front row from left:* Elvis, Shanna Tobin, Mary Lou Hammer, Kay Hardy, Carlene Martindell, Hazel Ann Linke, Dottie Vernieu, Jennifer Thurston, Dorothy Jones. *Back row from left:* Mary Anne Bushnell, Kari Peterson, Cathleen Sparrow, Juanita Watts, Lucille Niklason, Barbara Hoekstra.

CREATING A HEALTHIER COMMUNITY

McKay-Dee Hospital and various organizations work together to provide the community with healthcare education, as well as awareness and safety programs and events. Volunteers support these efforts at the hospital and out in the community. Some efforts are continual, while others are annual or scheduled through schools and other groups. All work to reduce preventable issues and increase wellness in both body and mind.

THE COMMUNITY HEALTH INFORMATION CENTER

The McKay-Dee Hospital Foundation and Volunteer Auxiliary support the Community Health Information Center (CHIC) in Intermountain McKay-Dee Hospital. The center is chock-full of free pamphlets, as well as books, videos, audiotapes, and equipment available for checkout by members of the community. Thousands of area residents use the facility each year so they can learn about various health topics, ranging from heart disease to hernias to headaches.

A computer program offers basic information about prescription drugs and their effects. Another computer program itemizes informational articles, medical journals and other

Mary Brian volunteers her time at the Children's Health Connection, which is supported by the McKay-Dee Hospital Foundation.

publications on various health topics so they can be printed out or found in the hospital's medical library. The CHIC center also has access to information on other resources in the community. It features a bulletin board posted with community events, support groups, and wellness classes. It also posts notices of safety checks, such as making sure a baby's car seat has been properly installed, or can help schedule an appointment with a Certified Child Passenger Safety Technician. In 2009, such technicians checked 376 car seats, loaned 49 car beds to families with low-birthweight babies, and gave 49 car seats to low-income families. The center also offers information on CPR, first aid, and babysitting-certification classes. CPR mannequins and health models are available for checkout. The models make great visuals for health fairs, science fairs, and other presentations.

Organizations can ask CHIC for help in finding and setting up guest speakers on health-related topics. The McKay-Dee Hospital Center Speakers Bureau offers presentations for free to groups of at least 30.

Physicians and other professionals can speak on mental health and emotional wellness, cancer, women's health issues, heart health, nutrition, stress and time management, sleep disorders, exercise and fitness, and more.

CHIC also sponsors Lite Lunch Learning Seminars on various health topics, such as headaches. The monthly hour-long events are held in the hospital's Education Auditorium. In 2009, more than 880 people attended presentations.

MAKING HEALTH CONNECTIONS

McKay-Dee Hospital and others work hard to sustain Annie Taylor Dee's legacy of wellness in the community and providing care to those who can't afford it.

The Health Connections program began in 1999 to meet the needs of patients in Northern Utah who might otherwise lack access to healthcare. The Utah Department of Health underscored this critical need by identifying Ogden's long history of culturally diverse residents who struggle with poverty, functional illiteracy, and a lack of healthcare. Through the combined efforts of Intermountain McKay-Dee Hospital Center, the McKay-Dee Foundation, the Junior League of Ogden, Midtown Community Health Center, and other community entities, the Health Connections program provides increased access to healthcare, decreased cost, and increased quality.

Children's Health Connection

Hundreds of healthcare volunteers team up for the annual Children's Health Connection fair over a two-day period to serve thousands of low-income children. Just before the school year starts, for the past 10 years, health issues have been identified for children of families who don't have a regular primary-care physician, are underinsured, or are uninsured. When health problems are identified, follow-up medical care is provided. In 2010, its 10th year, Children's Health Connection was coordinated and supported in cooperation with the Junior League of Ogden and Midtown Community Health Center. Children's Health Connection served 4,000 people, including 2,184 children, in 2009, an increase of 200 over 2008. More than 600 healthcare professionals and Ogden community members volunteer to provide no-cost physical exams, immunizations, and dental, vision, hearing, scoliosis, and developmental screenings. The event also provides free prescriptions, socks, underwear, haircuts, and school supplies. In 2005, the bilingual program was awarded the American Hospital Association's NOVA Shining Star award honoring effective, collaborative programs focused on improving community health status.

Women's Health Connection

More than 500 women a year receive no-charge cervical and breast cancer, oral, depression and other screenings. A women's support group is part of the program, which was started as a

Above, from left: Jennifer Berghout, RN, Pediatrics, Sally Jones, Community Projects Coordinator, and Danielle Nef, RN, discuss Children's Health Connection.

natural extension of the Children's Health Connection because healthy children need healthy moms to care for them.

Senior Health Connection

Registered nurses visit 14 area senior centers to answer questions, conduct blood pressure and cholesterol tests, check medications, determine bone density, assess foot care, and make physician recommendations. Four times each year, seniors are invited to the hospital for similar care. The program offers information on nutrition, dental care, pharmacy care, and more, and encourages seniors to become active and socialize. It also serves as a resource on services ranging from bus schedules to hospice care.

Child Life

Specialists provide "play therapy" to ensure that each child feels safe in the hospital. (It is the only such program north of Salt Lake City.)

Teen Suicide Awareness Walk

NUHOPE – the Northern Utah Hope task force – promotes healthy physical and behavioral lifestyles to combat teen suicides in Northern Utah. Programs are presented to Weber County high schools and encourage school-based suicide-prevention and education programs.

Developmental Screening Clinic

This program helps parents of children six months to six years establish developmental benchmarks and find referrals to appropriate community resources. Newborn Intensive Care Unit babies are also screened while still in the hospital.

Weber Coalition for a Healthy Community

The coalition provides coordination among other agencies to determine needs and the best use of resources. Established in 1999, it aims to improve healthcare access for uninsured or underinsured residents. It addresses suicide prevention, obesity, substance abuse, and more.

Midtown Community Health Center

Sponsored in part by Intermountain Healthcare, Midtown Community Health Center and the James Madison Elementary Health Center provide increased healthcare access to underserved populations.

> *Intermountain Healthcare has a long-held commitment to improve healthcare services for low-income and uninsured people in the community. We applaud McKay-Dee's continued support of Health Connections and recognize the events as effective health intervention.*
> *—John Pingree, Intermountain Healthcare,*
> *Vice President of Community Benefit*

The Dr. W.C. Swanson Family Foundation Child Development Center

The Swanson Foundation generously supports special projects that make a difference in the lives of families, including the Child Development Center built on the McKay-Dee Hospital campus. The center offers quality child care in a safe, clean, child-appropriate facility, making McKay-Dee one of the few employers in the state to open onsite daycare for the children of employees. The Swanson Foundation covered the entire $1.2 million in construction costs for the 9,000-square-foot facility and its playground to benefit more than 120 children.

A ribbon-cutting ceremony celebrates the grand opening on March 12, 2002, of the Dr. W.C. Swanson Child Development Center, a freestanding building at the north entrance of the Intermountain McKay-Dee Hospital Center campus. *From left:* Tom Hanrahan, McKay-Dee Hospital Administrator; Joey Hansen, Executive Director, McKay-Dee Hospital Foundation; Charles Swanson, Trustee of the Dr. W.C. Swanson Family Foundation; and Karen Burnett, Director of McKay-Dee Hospital Human Resources. The two young girls lending a hand are about to enjoy the new play area.

The Annie Taylor Dee Guest Home

As the hospital celebrates its 100th anniversary, another ambitious project supported by the McKay-Dee Hospital Foundation and generous donors was completed — a low-cost or free "home away from home" for families of patients receiving critical care at McKay-Dee.

The Annie Taylor Dee Guest Home is directly across the parking lot from Intermountain McKay-Dee Hospital and replaces three guest houses adjacent to the former hospital campus.

The 16,000-square-foot, two-level guest home includes community areas, including a meditation garden, outdoor deck and patio, a library with computers and Internet access, a living room, and laundry facilities.

Fourteen private guest suites will each accommodate up to four adults, and four of the suites adjoin to create larger suites for up to eight adults when needed. Portable cribs are available, and four suites are wheelchair accessible. Each guest suite includes two queen-size beds, private bathroom, television, table with chairs, and a kitchenette with a small sink, a microwave and a refrigerator.

Janice and the late Thomas D. Dee II made the lead gift to construct the home, and other Dee family members, hospital employees and other donors have contributed funds to assist in constructing and equipping the facility. The project is completely dependent on philanthropic support. The McKay-Dee Hospital Foundation accepted a challenge to raise $3 million for the facility and to create an endowment of $500,000 for operations and charitable lodging. Intermountain Healthcare provided the land.

The McKay-Dee Foundation broke ground July 30, 2009, for the 14-suite Annie Taylor Dee Guest Home, exactly 100 years to the month that Annie Taylor Dee broke ground on the original Thomas D. Dee Memorial Hospital.

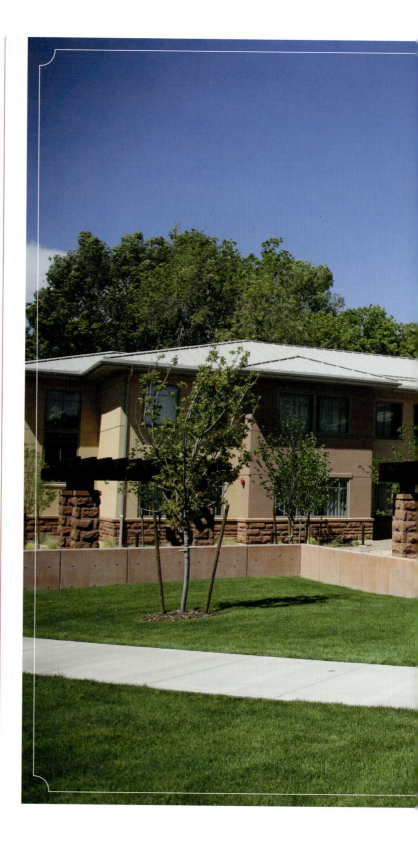

The idea of guest hospitality developed more than 25 years ago when a physician released a newborn from the NICU but the infant and mother couldn't return home to Wyoming because daily follow-up procedures were required. The family had no friends or family in the area to stay with, and no hotels or motels were conveniently located near the hospital. McKay-Dee's Social Services Department created a makeshift hotel room in the hospital so the mother could have "a home away from home" while her baby grew stronger. After that, compassionate hospital employees volunteered — often on short notice — to let patient families stay with them in their homes.

About 20 years ago, the hospital acquired three homes near its former campus to house families with members receiving critical care. In 2006 and 2007, the Hospital Social Services Department placed 1,147 guests in the homes. During those two years, the average stay was eight to 10 days, and the average number of guests on any given day was 14 to 16. Since opening the homes to guests, more than 10,000 people have had a place to stay during emergencies or inclement weather, or because of the inability to drive.

Though the Women's Council generously refurbished the homes in 2006, the structures, nearing 50 years old, still required major renovations and repairs. The hospital decided accommodations closer to its new campus would be more convenient for both McKay-Dee Hospital and its patients' families. Operating a single facility on campus will reduce challenges regarding registering guests, servicing the accommodations and providing security.

Offering a more relaxed environment also reinforces the hospital's commitment to a quality healing environment for patients and their families. The facility's design will help relieve the stress of a difficult situation and make guests and patients feel safe, welcome, and at ease during a time of crisis.

The guest suites at the Annie Taylor Dee Guest Home are decorated almost like a five-star hotel and each includes a kitchenette. In most instances, a nominal charge is requested to cover cleaning and maintenance.

The Ogden Surgical-Medical Society

For a time beginning in 1897, a group of physicians calling itself the Ogden Medical-Surgical Association leased a building from the city and called it Ogden General Hospital, though newspapers of the time referred to it as OMS Hospital. The hospital closed in 1910 when the Dee opened.

During World War II, medical training was limited because so many Ogden physicians were serving in far-flung military theaters and wartime conditions restricted travel. In 1946, realizing the acute need to keep abreast of medical advancements, three Ogden physicians — Drs. George M. Fister, Ezekiel R. Dumke, and Clark L. Rich, all associated with the Thomas D. Dee Memorial Hospital — started an annual medical conference somewhat reminiscent of the Ogden Medical-Surgical Association. They called the conference the Ogden Surgical-Medical Society.

Today, the conference continues to attract renowned medical practitioners and scientists. Dr. David Mechanic, the director of the Institute for Health, Healthcare Policy and Aging Research at Rutgers, spoke at the 2010 Ogden Surgical-Medical Society Conference. He raised the alarm, saying students are no longer interested in being a "first-stop doc" because of lower pay, higher medical school debt, longer days, administrative headaches, and the pressure to spend less one-on-one time with patients.

With health reform passed in 2010, the future in medicine faces many uncertainties. With every American being required to purchase insurance in the coming years, more primary-care physicians will need to be available to serve the resulting increase in patients.

Dr. Mechanic had several suggestions that would make family practice, or primary care, more attractive to students: allowing doctors to spend more time with patients, shifting to electronic medical records, and reimbursing based on the

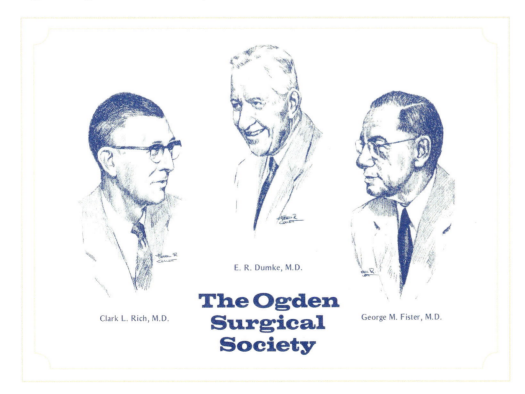

E. R. Dumke, M.D.

Clark L. Rich, M.D.

The Ogden Surgical Society

George M. Fister, M.D.

Dr. Clark L. Rich, Dr. Ezekiel R. Dumke, and Dr. George M. Fister, all associated with the Dee in 1946, began annual meetings so physicians could keep abreast of medical advancements during wartime, as training and travel were limited. The Ogden Surgical-Medical Society still meets annually to address issues of the day. Portraits by Farrell R. Collett.

"Why that hick town?"

The implication of this story and the international stature of the man who told it sum up the stature achieved by The Ogden Surgical-Medical Society's annual scientific meetings and their impact on the quality of medical care in the Intermountain West.

Sir Rodney Maingot, surgeon at the Royal Free Hospital in London, England, and a featured speaker in 1955, related the following story:

While on his way to Ogden, Dr. Maingot stopped in New York City and was engaged in conversation with a prominent East Coast physician.

"Where are you bound?" said the East Coast medical luminary.

"To Ogden, Utah, to address a surgical meeting," replied Dr. Maingot.

"Why that hick town?" the East Coast doctor replied.

"That's quite a meeting they have out there," Dr. Maingot said. "Cattell, Ochsner and Backus have spoken there, and if it's good enough for them, it ought to be good enough for me."

The East Coast physician thought awhile and then said wistfully, "Wonder why I've never been invited?"

"Maybe you haven't arrived yet," said Dr. Maingot.

From the Ogden Surgical-Medical Society's official history, 1946 to 2005.

The Salt Lake Tribune

MORNING AND SUNDAY
SALT LAKE CITY 10, UTAH

May 8, 1967

Dr. George M. Fister,
1680-29th St.,
Ogden, Utah

Dear Dr. Fister:

I started medical writing at about the same time the Ogden Surgical Society was organized, and I have found its annual meetings to be a rich source of material for medical articles of interest and value to the public.

All of the meetings--and I have "covered" each one for The Tribune--have been of very high quality, as far as scientific content is concerned. In addition they have offered social events of an appealing nature. One thing that must not be forgotten is the genuine friendliness shown always by the Ogden doctors and their wives. It has been notable that the speakers, almost without exception, have said how pleased they were to be invited to Ogden. I am sure these have been sincere expressions.

I feel the Ogden Surgical Society meetings are among Utah's chief medical assets, and that the state owes a debt of gratitude to the townspeople and other supporters, as well as to members of the society.

Sincerely yours,

William C. Patrick
Medical Editor

The *Salt Lake Tribune*'s medical writer, William G. Patrick, lauded the Ogden Surgical Society in this 1967 letter.

performance of medical personnel — not quantity of care.

Intermountain McKay-Dee Hospital Center has long been a model for the future of medical care and has already implemented many of Mechanic's suggestions, making the future of medical care in Ogden in the face of healthcare reform less uncertain.

INTERMOUNTAIN HEALTHCARE AND MCKAY-DEE: MODELS FOR THE COUNTRY

In 1991, Intermountain Healthcare, of which McKay-Dee is a member, was presented the Healthcare Forum/Witt Award. The annual award is presented based on commitment to improving quality of healthcare. According to a McKay-Dee employee newsletter from August 1991, McKay-Dee and all other Intermountain Healthcare hospitals were among the first to conduct research in improving the quality of medical procedures. It defined quality for employees and set guidelines for quality improvement. The Total Quality Management approach guidelines set out the steps:

1) Conduct a detailed study of the processes involved in delivering healthcare, and relate the processes to carefully measured outcomes;

2) Establish the best way to perform the process;

3) Eliminate inappropriate variations from the process; and

4) Document improvements in quality — the medical outcomes.

Hospital Administrator Thomas Hanrahan wrote in the newsletter that Intermountain Healthcare is internationally recognized as a leader in quality management. A hospital Total Quality Management Council, whose members are administrative managers and department heads, volunteer teams of physicians and employees from almost every area of the hospital, continually look at medical processes and systems, making changes to enhance quality of care as needed.

As quality improves, Hanrahan wrote, costs decline. Perhaps the seed of this success was planted in the 1980s by an Intermountain Healthcare pulmonologist who wrote a protocol for treating a condition, setting recommendations based on previous successful treatments. One after another, other hospital departments followed suit with their cases.

Using this technique, Intermountain Healthcare reduced preterm deliveries, Newborn Intensive Care Unit admissions, adverse drug events, death rates, and readmission rates, according to the November 2009 *New York Times Magazine.*

In 1993, five Intermountain Healthcare representatives were invited to participate in meetings of President Bill Clinton's National Health Care Reform Task Force. One of the president's top healthcare advisors said the Clinton administration viewed Intermountain Healthcare as a national model for healthcare reform.

In the January 1993 issue of *Quality Matters*, a national health industry publication, Dr. Kenneth Thorpe — President Clinton's healthcare advisor and an associate professor of health policy and administration at the University of North Carolina at Chapel Hill — said hospitals would do well to learn more about Intermountain Healthcare and its enduring quality during cost reductions.

"If you look at types of health plans, Intermountain Healthcare is a fabulous system. It studies what is effective and ineffective and it acts on it. I think systems like Intermountain Healthcare will be right at the forefront," he said.

Steve Kohlert, Intermountain Healthcare Senior Vice President, agreed in a January 1993 hospital newsletter to employees. "... The new administration seems to be leaning toward community health networks that unite hospitals, physicians and insurers around a concept of patient-centered care. Intermountain Healthcare has been doing this for years."

That year, Intermountain Healthcare President Scott

Parker was named one of the Top 50 national leaders in healthcare reform by *Modern Healthcare Magazine*. The magazine said: "The individuals are helping to shape, or will be important in coming efforts to modify, the nation's healthcare financing and delivery system."

Under Thomas Hanrahan's leadership, McKay-Dee began patient-focused care in 1993. Caregivers were trained to provide a wider scope of services so patients see fewer caregivers and can receive more direct care in their rooms from small teams, reducing the need for time-consuming and necessary coordination and paperwork. The team brought clinical, business, ancillary, and support services to patients rather than bringing patients to various services.

The July 1993 employee newsletter stated: "In order to allow people to contribute ideas without fear of losing employment, the hospital has made a commitment that no individual will lose employment as a result of this project."

All were welcome and encouraged to offer ideas. A Steering Committee was set up to oversee seven design teams who fielded employees' suggestions and worked intensively to figure out how to reorganize their areas around the patient.

President Clinton's healthcare reform efforts may not have been successful, but President Barack Obama's were. In 2009 and 2010, the issue of healthcare reform divided the nation and Congress. Ultimately, healthcare reform prevailed, with President Obama holding Intermountain Healthcare up as a model for the rest of the country, just as President Clinton did years before him.

Intermountain Healthcare hospital administrators feel confident about the transitions that healthcare reform presents because Intermountain Healthcare's traditions of continual improvement in hospital facilities, patient care, and costs have already poised its facilities, including McKay-Dee Hospital Center, ahead of the curve.

In the April 2010 Intermountain Healthcare newsletter, Greg Poulsen, Intermountain Healthcare's Senior Vice President, said, "The goal of the legislation over time is to encourage organizations to go to what's being called an accountable care organization concept. It's the concept of physicians and hospitals and other caregivers working together to meet the needs of the patient. That's been part of our DNA for 20 years or more."

He goes on to say the legislation will affect other organizations more than Intermountain Healthcare because Intermountain Healthcare's focus and direction are already where reform is aiming for changes.

As far as the increase in patients because of the requirement that every American be insured by 2014, Intermountain Healthcare's Poulsen says, "We're already acting as the safety net provider for our state, which means that the majority of people that don't have insurance today end up in our clinics and our facilities. ... We're already doing a lot of those volumes that will come ultimately. ... I can't think of anybody in the country that's so well-positioned to meet these new challenges as we are."

In fact, in June 2009, *U.S. News & World Report's* Health Research Rankings & Advice website ranked the top hospitals in the country. Intermountain McKay-Dee Hospital was among them, based on a year's worth of patient surveys compiled by the American Hospital Association.

Eighty-four percent of patients said they would definitely recommend Intermountain McKay-Dee Hospital to their family and friends. The state average was 71 percent; the national average was 68 percent.

Seventy-four percent of McKay-Dee patients said they were highly satisfied with their hospital visit. The state average was 66 percent; the national average was 64 percent.

In 2009, President Barack Obama held Intermountain Healthcare — made up of 23 hospitals, including McKay-Dee — up to the nation as a model.

"We have to ask why places like Intermountain Health (sic) in Salt Lake City can offer high-quality care at costs well below average, but other places in America can't," President Obama pointed out.

"We need to identify the best practices across the country, learn from the success and replicate that success elsewhere. And we should change the warped incentives that reward doctors and hospitals based on how many tests or procedures they prescribe, even if those tests or procedures aren't necessary or result from medical mistakes. Doctors across this country did not get into the medical profession to be bean counters or paper pushers, to be lawyers or business executives. They became doctors to heal people. And that's what we must free them to do."

Utah had the lowest per-capita healthcare spending rate in the nation at $3,972 when the national average was $7,026. Intermountain executives say, when controlled for age and health status, Utah also performs well at lower costs, said Intermountain Healthcare's Poulsen. He attributes that to the organization's team approach, which cuts down on unnecessary tests and medication errors.

"In Intermountain Healthcare and in Utah, we're focused on evidence-based medicine, and we're more able to provide only the services our patients need," he told the *Salt Lake Tribune*. "The result is, utilization is lower here, outcomes are better, and costs are dramatically lower. A growing number of healthcare and national leaders are seeing those results, and it's very nice that the president is among them."

A 100-year evolution of model healthcare at McKay-Dee Hospital

 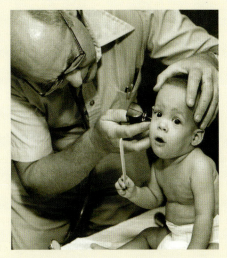 

↦ CELEBRATING 100 YEARS ↤

I NTERMOUNTAIN MCKAY-DEE CELEBRATED ITS 100TH ANNIVERSARY AND ANNIE TAYLOR DEE'S LEGACY IN A NUMBER OF WAYS IN 2010. IT CUT THE RIBBON TO THE NEW ANNIE TAYLOR DEE GUEST HOME, STARTING A NEW WAY TO CONTINUE A STRONG SERVICE FOR PATIENTS AND THEIR FAMILIES.

The McKay-Dee Hospital Foundation held a black-tie 100th anniversary event at the Ogden Eccles Conference Center to help raise funds for the guest home. During the celebration, the foundation honored individuals, employees, donors, and organizations that have contributed to the hospital's success over the past 100 years. About 700 community members in black ties and gowns helped celebrate the hospital's amazing history. Decorations featured historical moments of health-care in the area, which added an amazing ambiance to the ballroom. The program featured speakers, employees, donors, and organizations that have contributed to the success of the hospital during the past 100 years. A video featuring hundreds of people born at the Dee or McKay-Dee Hospital illustrated the thousands of people in the community who are proud to call themselves a Dee or McKay-Dee baby. The program continued with videos and speakers featuring memories of original Dee nurses, doctors, volunteers, past administrators,

and contributors. The evening captivated the audience and reminded everyone of the importance of those who sacrificed and built an amazing organization over the last 100 years. Donations from the gala raised more than $60,000 to benefit the new Annie Taylor Dee Guest Home.

The hospital hosted a 5K Run, Walk or Crawl in June that started at the Thomas D. Dee Memorial Hospital park — the site of the original hospital — at 24th Street and Harrison Boulevard, wound through the site of the second hospital, and finished at the new Intermountain McKay-Dee Hospital Center campus at 4401 Harrison Boulevard. Afterward, next to the hospital's scenic pond, breakfast was served — even to those who didn't expend any calories beforehand; race participation was not required in order to enjoy the food.

A special exhibit was held at Ogden's Union Station. It featured a coloring contest and design-an-ad contest by area schoolchildren, who played up the hospital's 100 years of high-quality medical care in the community. Professional artists from the area also submitted pieces that ranged from purely medical to spiritually comforting to maternal to historical. Many of the paintings are to be on permanent display at the hospital.

Art pieces weren't the only things in the exhibit that addressed history. Displays depicting the evolution of healthcare included: nursing uniforms from the early 1900s; a registration book from the Dee; circa-1900 laryngoscopic set, birthing straps, umbilical-cord cutter, breast pump, ophthalmic surgical set, tonsillectomy set, and more; the five-paneled mural celebrating the life of the late LDS Church President David O. McKay, who helped save the Dee in 1914-15 and for whom the hospital is named today; and the key to the hospital's front door that was presented to McKay at the 1969 dedication ceremony.

Farr Better Ice Cream also got in on the act by creating a flavor just for McKay-Dee's 100th anniversary — and just in time for summer. The vanilla, nutty, caramelly-flavored ice cream was named "McKay-Dee's Churn of the Century" after hospital employees submitted their suggestions.

McKay-Dee also created a 100th anniversary coloring book for young patients and hospital visitors, and created a 100th anniversary logo that decorated cups, bottled water, menus, napkins, staff uniforms, items in the gift shop, and other products. The logo also decorated items featured at hospital-sponsored events, such as the Ogden Marathon and other races in town, the Ogden Pioneer Days & Rodeo, Business After Hours Chamber of Commerce gatherings, the Ogden Surgical-Medical Society Conference, gatherings for physicians and their families, and more.

This special coffee-table book was produced to capture the fulfillment of Annie Taylor Dee's dream to memorialize her husband, Thomas Duncombe Dee, after his death in 1905. The book pays tribute to those who helped advance medical care in Ogden, through financial means or through offering their time, talents, and service since the Dee opened in 1910

and as the hospital grew and changed locations.

The hospital also has asked people to share their memories of Thomas D. Dee Memorial Hospital, McKay-Dee Hospital, and Intermountain McKay-Dee Hospital Center. The comments could show up in hospital publications and promotions. There are sure to be many, as a good portion of longtime Utah residents were born or have received care in one of the three facilities.

Almost as a topping to the anniversary cake, Intermountain Healthcare's McKay-Dee Hospital Center was named one of the nation's Top 100 hospitals by Thomson Reuters, a leading provider of information and solutions to improve the cost and quality of healthcare. The award recognizes hospitals that have achieved excellence in clinical outcomes, patient safety, and patient satisfaction, as well as financial performance and operation efficiency.

The top hospitals were identified through an in-depth analysis of 2,926 short-term, acute-care, nonfederal hospitals in 10 areas: mortality, medical complications, patient safety, average length of stay, expenses, profitability, patient satisfaction, adherence to clinical standards of care, and post-discharge mortality and readmission rates for heart attack, heart failure, and pneumonia.

Intermountain McKay-Dee Hospital Center and the nation's other Top 99 hospitals were featured in the March 2010 edition of *Modern Healthcare* magazine.

In its 100th year, McKay-Dee aims to keep up its standards through implementing lean manufacturing principles that it calls i², or Innovate and Improve. The hospital aims to work with hospital employees to determine how to make patient care more efficient and cost effective. McKay-Dee is creating a culture of ideas with the belief that no one knows how to do a job better than the person performing it, says Tim Pehrson, CEO of McKay-Dee. "It's reducing patient dissatisfaction and costs by making the work force part of the solution," he says.

"As Washington and hospitals across the nation strive

to reform healthcare, no one will be better poised than Intermountain Healthcare, precisely because of our continuous improvement efforts," Pehrson says. "i² is a formal methodology for eliminating nonvalue-added work from hospital processes, thereby improving cost, quality, and service to patients. Hospital employees have sought the advice of experts and organizations – including Autoliv and OC Tanner – and have found success in applying these lean manufacturing principles."

Employees recommend ideas that best apply to the hospital and put them into motion, creating a best-practice checklist to guide them in better serving patients and the community.

Pehrson says it is this hardwiring of process improvements into the daily work of hospital employees that helps the hospital continually improve and follow Intermountain Healthcare's vision of providing extraordinary care.

"If Annie Taylor Dee could see what her vision has become in 2010," Pehrson says, "she would surely be proud, because Intermountain McKay-Dee Hospital Center isn't just improving medical care in Northern Utah, which was her initial goal; it is helping to improve medical care across the country by being held up as a model for other hospitals to emulate."

One hundred years later, several governmental agencies, including the U.S. Congress, have acknowledged Annie Taylor Dee's vision that has become today's Intermountain McKay-Dee Hospital Center.

IV

111TH CONGRESS
2D SESSION

H. RES. 1136

Recognizing the 100th anniversary of the establishment of the McKay-Dee Hospital in northern Utah.

IN THE HOUSE OF REPRESENTATIVES

MARCH 3, 2010

Mr. BISHOP of Utah (for himself, Mr. CHAFFETZ, and Mr. MATHESON) submitted the following resolution; which was referred to the Committee on Energy and Commerce

---

RESOLUTION

Recognizing the 100th anniversary of the establishment of the McKay-Dee Hospital in northern Utah.

Whereas McKay-Dee Hospital and its predecessors have offered 100 years of continuous health care service to the residents of northern Utah from 1910 to 2010;

Whereas tens of thousands of hardworking individuals have devoted their lives to the care, concern, and healing of patients at the three hospitals that have become Intermountain McKay-Dee Hospital and Medical Center;

Whereas hundreds of thousands of Utah residents have received medical care during McKay-Dee's 100 years of service;

2

Whereas McKay-Dee Hospital represents the fulfillment of Annie Taylor Dee's dream to provide access to high quality health care for the residents of northern Utah;

Whereas McKay-Dee Hospital's contributions to the community at-large come in many more ways than simply providing traditional hospital-based health care services;

Whereas every Dee, McKay, and McKay-Dee facility has offered innovative medical technology; and

Whereas Intermountain Healthcare was recently recognized as a national model for providing quality and affordable healthcare: Now, therefore, be it

1   *Resolved*, That the House of Representatives—

2   (1) recognizes the 100th anniversary of the es-

3   tablishment of the McKay-Dee Hospital in northern

4   Utah; and

5   (2) commends McKay-Dee Hospital and its em-

6   ployees for providing quality care to hundreds of

7   thousands of patients over the last century.

○

•HRES 1136 IH

The United States Congress recognized McKay-Dee Hospital for its 100th anniversary. Utah's three U.S. Congressmen, Rob Bishop, First District, R-Utah; Jim Matheson, Second District, D-Utah; and Jason Chaffetz, Third District, R-Utah, sponsored the above resolution.

The Public Relations department of Intermountain McKay-Dee Hospital Center wishes to acknowledge the help of Intermountain Healthcare personnel and the McKay-Dee Foundation personnel's research support for access to archives in the assembly and review of materials for this book.

A History of the Ogden Surgical-Medical Society 1946 to 2005
Compiled by Val B. Johnson, MD

A Tradition of Caring: A History of the Thomas D. Dee Memorial Hospital and McKay-Dee Hospital Center
1910–1982
by Eleanor B. Moler

Brief History of the Thomas D. Dee Memorial Hospital 1913–1915
Excerpt from Hospital History compiled by Barbara Dirks

Building a Dynasty: The Story of the Thomas D. Dee Family
1987
by Eleanor B. Moler

Centuries of Progress
Stepping Stones for Healthcare in the New Millennium Historical Highlights
Thomas D. Dee Memorial Hospital–David O. McKay Hospital
McKay-Dee Hospital Center
Thomas D. Dee Memorial Hospital School of Nursing

Dee Memorial Hospital and Nurses Training School
1915–1919, 1920–1955
Foundation Archives

Dee Memorial Hospital Nurses Alumni Association History
Member booklet

"Weber County's History"
by Richard Sadler and Richard C. Roberts, 2000, commissioned by the Weber County Commission

First-person interviews conducted by Caroll Shreeve and Stephen G. Handy of current and former McKay-Dee Hospital administrators, doctors, nurses, and other medical personnel.

McKay-Dee Hospital Foundation History/Women's Council History
Compiled by Barbara Dirks
1992–1993

McKay-Dee Hospital Annual Reports by departments and service groups
Public Relations department archives

McKay-Dee Hospital History
Compiled by Barbara Dirks
1971

McKay-Dee Hospital Scanner newsletters
1969 to 1990

McKay-Dee Volunteer Auxiliary Historical Archives

Ogden Standard-Examiner newspaper archives
Weber County Library microfiche archives

The History of Medicine in Weber County from 1952 to 1980

The Story of Intermountain Healthcare
by Tom Vitelli
1995

Weber State University Special Collections
Dee Family and Dee Hospital Archives
Photos, letters, and miscellaneous documents